30 DAYS TO Taming YOUR Kid's Tongue

Deborah Smith Pegues

HARVEST HOUSE PUBLISHERS
EUGENE, OREGON

Cover design by Koechel Peterson & Associates, Inc., Minneapolis, Minnesota

Cover photos © iStock, Polka Dot, Digital Vision / Thinkstock

The names in the stories that appear throughout this book have been changed to protect personal identities.

30 DAYS TO TAMING YOUR KID'S TONGUE
Copyright © 2014 by Deborah Smith Pegues
Published by Harvest House Publishers
Eugene, Oregon 97402
www.harvesthousepublishers.com

Library of Congress Cataloging-in-Publication Data
Pegues, Deborah Smith, 1950- author.
    30 days to taming your kid's tongue / Deborah Smith Pegues.
        pages cm
    Includes bibliographical references.
    ISBN 978-0-7369-5829-5 (pbk.)
    ISBN 978-0-7369-5830-1 (eBook)
    1. Oral communication—Religious aspects—Christianity. 2. Interpersonal communication—Religious aspects—Christianity. 3. Parenting—Religious aspects—Christianity. 4. Children—Conduct of life. I. Title. II. Title: Thirty days to taming your kid's tongue.
    BV4597.53.C64P438 2014
    248.8'45--dc23
                                                                    2014000908

Printed in the United States of America

14 15 16 17 18 19 20 21 22 23 / BP-JH / 10 9 8 7 6 5 4 3 2 1

This book is dedicated to parents who desire to develop their children into polite, polished, positive, personable, and powerful communicators.

Acknowledgments

Nobody accomplishes any worthwhile objective without the help of people—good, caring, qualified people committed to getting the job done. That was my experience on this project. Special thanks to Darla Noble, my resident parenting expert and key researcher. Your input was invaluable. So was that of Yvetta Franklin, Patricia Ashley, Darlene Moss, Pamela Kelley, Delisa Kelley, Roberta Morris, Carolyn Ratliff, Elizabeth Mirr Wysocki, Dr. Saundra Dalton Smith, Frank Robinson, and Greg and Teresa McCurry.

My prayer squad played a major role in my productivity and focus. Thank you Pastor Edward and Vanessa Smith, Renee Hernandez, Billie Rodgers, Yvonne Johnson, Cheryl Martin, Diane Gardner, Marva Sykes, Sylvia Gardner, and Josie Martin. Jeanette Stone and the women in my Zoe Christian Fellowship of Whittier Life Group stayed on the wall interceding for this project to the very end. Thank you for your faithfulness and love.

My social media friends were awesome with their support…stories, personal experiences, insights, and prayers. Thank you to all you parents who offered your input.

As always, I'm grateful to my Harvest House Publishers dream team: President Bob Hawkins Jr., acquisitions editor Terry Glaspey, senior editor Rod Morris, and the rest of the crew. Thank you for your never ending ideas and the awesome job you do in getting the books into the marketplace. Your unwavering commitment to the Scriptures as a guide for everyday living is inspiring. Thank you for your high standards of excellence in every aspect of publishing.

Finally, there is no superlative adequate to express my appreciation to my husband, Darnell. The man is tailor-made for me and my divine purpose. What a joy to be married for over thirty-five years to such an adaptable, fun-loving, handsome, balanced, self-sufficient, and supportive mate. I'm eternally grateful to God for such an asset.

Contents

Part Two: Triumphing Over Negative Communication

Prologue

"Old School" Standards, "New School" Strategies

I am not a parent or a psychologist. I'm a self-proclaimed "professional people watcher"; a woman on a mission to help people communicate better. So relax. This book is not a truckload of "shoulds" to make you feel guilty about how you are managing the hardest job on the planet—raising kids. Also know that I will not subject you to a bunch of incomprehensible psychobabble (truth is, I don't know any) about how kids need the freedom to do whatever their little hearts desire. I do marvel, however, at how modern parents jumped on the bandwagon during the sixties and started giving more credibility to child-development "experts" than to folks like Susanna Wesley, who birthed nineteen children. Her sons, John and Charles, were founding fathers of the Methodist Church. Parents who desired to raise godly children embraced Susanna's classic "rules" [1]—many of which found their way into our household and affected how I was raised.

I took responsibility at an early age for the frequent

care and feeding of my siblings. I'm the second oldest of seven children and the only girl. By the time I was seven, my mom had taught me how to make meals from scratch for the entire family, to clean house, and to use the old wringer-type washing machine without getting my arms caught between the rollers.

Corralling a bunch of rambunctious boys was no small task; conflicts were commonplace. But I learned a lot about effective communication (actually, I should say *ineffective* communication), a topic that has fascinated me for over a third of a century. I've managed difficult people as a former Fortune 500 financial executive and a nonprofit administrator. During the course of my career, I have taught many adults how to communicate directly and powerfully. I've been blessed to proclaim my message to millions through television and radio appearances, book sales, conferences, and private interventions.

After the tremendous response from around the world to my book *30 Days to Taming Your Tongue*, I realized that many adults have interpersonal communications difficulties that could have been resolved or minimized if they had been addressed in their early childhood. So, in a departure from teaching old dogs new tricks, I'm writing *30 Days to Taming Your Kid's Tongue* because I believe it pays to teach effective communication during the toddler-to-twelve period of a child's life.

By the time kids reach their teen years, their basic communication behavior is already entrenched; for many, their people skills are mediocre at best. I find this to be a real tragedy because every endeavor that anybody undertakes in life will require interaction with people. There is no way around it. We all need people to help us achieve our personal or professional goals. Thus, we have to be intentional in developing strong people skills to communicate our desires and to position ourselves where others are motivated to embrace and support us. This is why good home training is essential. Kids have to be taught what to say and what not to say, which behaviors inspire support from others and which do not.

This book is a combination of "old school" standards and "new school" strategies. I believe that kids can be well behaved and still be expressive. I believe that parents can administer the "rod of correction" in several forms— but always with love and consistency. Chip Ingram, a popular pastor and Bible teacher, agrees:

> When juvenile delinquents, as part of a research study, were asked how they knew their parents' feelings toward them, almost all of them said that lack of discipline in their home was a sign that their parents didn't love them. We often think that we're expressing love when we repeatedly say, "I'll give you another chance." What we're really doing, though, is neglecting to set boundaries that let our children know they're in a safety zone where they can feel secure. One of the most powerful ways to love your child is to be consistent in your discipline. And that's really hard. We're inclined to do whatever we can to maintain a friendship with our kids, when discipline is actually much more important.[2]

So, whether you chose spankings, lectures, denial of privileges, or other methods, kids need to know with certainty that bad behavior is a bad idea. (Even though I'm targeting the book to parents, know that I'm also including grandparents and other child raisers and influencers.)

In Part One, we'll look at strategies for training kids in the art of "Positive Communication"—from social courtesies and niceties to talking to God. In Part Two, I'll focus on "Triumphing over Negative Communication"—exchanges that you as a parent cannot afford to tolerate.

Caution: If you do not agree with some of my suggestions or think they won't work for your child, move on to the next one. One size never fits all. All I ask is that you not throw the baby out with the bathwater; just hear me out until the end.

I think you'll be glad you did.

Part One

Training in Positive Communication

Day 1

"Thank You"

"Ingratitude to man is ingratitude to God."
SAMUEL IBN NAGHRELA (993–1056),
JEWISH SCHOLAR AND POET

Story has it that when Uncle Bill offered Little Johnny an orange, he accepted it without a word.

"Little Johnny, what do you say?" his mother asked.

"Peel it!" he exclaimed.

Parents, teachers, and others who regularly work with children readily agree there is an *ingratitude epidemic* among today's young people. It seems that most parents have forgotten that teaching children to express appreciation for the gifts or kindnesses others extend to them is basic to good manners. It pays to begin early so that being thankful becomes a habit that follows your children throughout their entire lives. Here are just a few of the reasons why children must learn to say thank you:

- It subconsciously teaches them that they are not *entitled* to the things they are given.

- It teaches them to acknowledge another person's generosity or sacrifice on their behalf.

- It makes them more conscious of being man-
  nerly in other ways.

- It makes the giver feel good to be appreciated.

While you need to train your children to get into
the habit of expressing appreciation to others, it is more
important to teach them to develop a *heart* of gratitude.
To this end, some parents proactively expose their children to how the less fortunate live by taking them on a
trip to the disadvantaged side of town or the other side
of the world. They know how easy it is for their kids to
get comfortable in their little bubble of abundance and
develop an erroneous view of the real world.

One day Jesus healed ten men suffering from leprosy,
one of the most isolating and dreaded diseases of the day.
He expressed dismay when only one of them, who happened to be a foreigner, returned to say thank you.

> One of them, when he saw that he was healed,
> came back to Jesus, shouting, "Praise God!" He fell
> to the ground at Jesus' feet, thanking him for what he
> had done. This man was a Samaritan.
>
> Jesus asked, "Didn't I heal ten men? Where are the
> other nine? Has no one returned to give glory to God
> except this foreigner?" (Luke 17:15-18).

Good parents remind their children that every gift
comes from God (James 1:17); thus, when they are
ungrateful to others, they are actually ungrateful to God.

When you fail to teach your children to say thank
you, the consequences are always negative:

- It gives them the *false* impression that the world revolves around their needs, their desires, and their whims.

- It leaves a vacuum in their character where respect should be.

- It lessens their chances of making positive and influential first impressions.

- It makes them selfish and thoughtless when it comes to the rights and desires of others.

- It puts them at a greater risk for failed marriages and poor parent-child relationships.

- It lessens their chances for job advancement as an adult because they are unable or unwilling to express appreciation.

Manners matter, and there's no time like the present to make instilling them a priority in your child's life. Here are a few practical ways you can teach your children to make saying thank you part of their normal behavior:

- Be consistent in saying thank you to your children, your spouse, and everyone else in your circle of interaction.

- Expect and *require* your children to say thank you to you and anyone who compliments them or extends a kind deed to them. You may even have to prep small children before their birthday parties or special times to say thank you for every gift received. Even if they don't like the gift or already own a similar item, "thank you" is the only appropriate response. Teach them that they are not only thanking the person for the gift but for the effort in selecting it, buying it, and getting it to them.

- Affirm their use of thank you by responding, "You're welcome."

- Explain that being appreciated motivates people to continue their generosity.

- Read younger children stories like *The Berenstain Bears Forget Their Manners*.[1] This will give you an invitation to talk about the importance of manners.

Peter and Jeanette are the parents of a teenager and a preteen. Both parents are highly paid professionals and provide their children with all the luxuries and benefits that come from having financial abundance. While they give generously to their church and those in need, they are failing miserably to teach their children to be appreciative of the things they have. Instead of "Thank you" coming from the children, it's "Is that all?" or "That's not the one I wanted," or "Why can't I have both?"

When Jeanette announced to them that she had breast cancer and would be undergoing chemo for several months, her twelve-year-old asked, "We're still going to Florida, aren't we?" This is the attitude that Jill Rigby warns of in her inspirational parenting guide, *Raising Respectful Kids in a Disrespectful World*:

When your children begin to expect "things" from you, they lose their gratitude. Think of the daughter whose father travels frequently for his job. Because Dad feels guilty for being away, he brings his daughter a gift as a token of his love. But as time passes, she stops anticipating her father's return and, instead, anticipates the gift he will bring her. When the day comes that Dad doesn't bring a gift, the daughter is unhappy— with life and with her father. Parents who over-indulge their kids are nurturing ungratefulness in their children's hearts. The more things these parents give, the more things their kids want.[2]

While the focus of this book is on verbal communi-cation, I implore parents to preserve one of the lost arts of etiquette—written thank-you notes. When my friend Dee inherited a large sum of money from her late father, she decided to give a portion of the bounty to her nieces and nephews, the majority of whom were young adults. To her dismay, not one of them sent her a thank-you card. A couple of them did send her an email.

She was upset by what she considered their "gross ingratitude," and she expressed her disappointment to them in a group email. One of the parents downplayed the incident, reportedly telling her son, "Try to under-stand that a lot of older people are stuck on getting a written thank-you note when they give someone a pres-ent."

This mom missed a key teaching opportunity. The issue was not the idiosyncrasies of older people; it was about being grateful and appreciating and acknowledging a gift in a meaningful way. I've had the experience of mailing a young person a gift and never being told it was even received. How rude! I've known many generous benefactors who, feeling they've been taken for granted, cut off all gifts to certain recipients simply because they failed to show gratitude for their kindness with a thank-you note.

I recommend that parents keep a set of thank-you cards on hand and let their children see them modeling this habit from time to time. Children who can write can be encouraged to prepare their own notes when they receive a special gift. The note can be worded as simply as, "Thanks for the model car. It's really cool."

Remember, when you teach your *children* to be kind, compassionate, and thankful, you're preparing them to be kind, compassionate, and thankful *adults*.

Day 2

"Please"

*"Treat everyone with politeness, even
those who are rude to you—not because
they are nice, but because you are."*
AUTHOR UNKNOWN

Maggie has a habit of barking orders at the food servers when eating out: "Bring me some water." "We'd like some more bread!" "You can bring the check now." Frustrated by her rudeness, her friend Della follows up each of her commands with an overly dramatized "Pleeeeze." "Here is an adult who obviously never learned the importance of being polite to *everybody*," Della told me, "even to those in service positions." Oddly, Maggie is a generous tipper; she just doesn't think that saying "please" is important.

Not so for Daniel the young Israelite. In the account of his early life recorded in Daniel 1:1-15, we find him being socially and politically smart enough to exercise the power of please. King Nebuchadnezzar's army had captured Daniel, along with many other handsome and smart young Jewish boys, and brought them to Babylon to serve in the king's palace. When Daniel learned of the special diet they would have to follow as part of their preparation, he purposed in his heart that he was not going to defile himself with the king's non-kosher foods. As a captive, he had no leverage to negotiate his way out of the situation. Therefore, he politely requested that the supervisor of the training program grant special consideration to him and his three best friends:

> "Please test your servants for ten days, and let them give us vegetables to eat and water to drink. Then let our appearance be examined before you, and the appearance of the young men who eat the portion of the king's delicacies; and as you see fit, so deal with your servants." So he consented with them in this matter, and tested them ten days (Daniel 1:12-14 NKJV).

At the end of the ten days, Daniel and his friends proved to be healthier and better nourished than those who had eaten the non-kosher food. Therefore, the supervisor allowed them to continue their vegetarian diet. Imagine what the outcome would have been had Daniel not taken the polite approach.

What about you? In your daily interactions with others, including your family, do you *request* or *command* people to respond to your desires? Do you say please frequently? If not, could this be the reason your child may struggle with this important courtesy?

Parents, you simply *must* teach and expect your children to say please. You will exert a major influence in helping society to overcome the selfish, entitled mind-set that prevails in our culture. The effort must begin at home. Parents must begin to raise children who understand the value of *requesting* rather than *commanding*.

Several behavioral studies document that we have become a self-indulgent society, expecting and demanding what we want when we want it. These studies also show that parents are much to blame for this social decline due to their lack of instruction about manners.

Teaching children to say please is not as difficult as it may seem, especially if the training starts early. For parents of toddlers and preschoolers, it all comes down to expectations and consequences. If you say please and you instruct, expect, and *require* your children to say please, it will become second nature to them. If you don't make it a requirement with consistent consequences, you are going to produce very rude offspring.

Teach your kids that the word *please* is like a master key; it unlocks a person's willingness to hear their requests. By not teaching children to say please, parents unwittingly:

- minimize their respect for authority
- give their blessing to the whatever-I-say-is-okay mind-set
- add to the number of failed marriages due to a lack of appreciation and respect for one another

For parents whose children are a bit older and have already fallen into the habit of not being polite, the following suggestions should help you get them on a new path.

Tell your children that you're raising the bar for respect and that *please* must now become a household word.

Ignore any request not accompanied by the word please. You may have to remind them by saying something like, "I'm waiting for the magic word."

Set a good example by saying please to them ("Billy, will you please take the trash out before dinner?" "Gabby, please put the dog outside."). This will help you to give and gain respect from your kids. *Caution:* It may not be wise in some instances for you to say please as it could appear to weaken your authority or imply that compliance is optional. If you are giving critical instructions or commands, then stronger statements are in order:

"I need you to be in the house before dark."

"Stop kicking your brother."

"You must do your homework before watching TV."

However, a simple courtesy, such as "Please pass the butter" or "Please use your indoor voice," is just good home training.

During my childhood, I don't recall my often verbally abusive father or even my kindhearted mother ever saying please to any of us seven children. Everything was a command—and failure to perform the task my father commanded brought swift and painful consequences. *Please* was simply not part of our household culture. Over the years, I've often had to remind myself to add please to my requests. Sometimes I forget. Of course, my loving husband is quick to remind me when I do. For example, when I ask, "Could you bring my briefcase upstairs?" he will typically reply, "Please?"

Explain to your children that saying please helps others feel appreciated since saying it shows that you recognize the other person has the choice to grant your request (even though in some circumstances the other person may suffer negative consequences if he does not comply).

Teach them that saying please to others shows humility and respect and will likely garner them more respect, cooperation, and favor in return. Of course, you must caution that saying please should not be done with a motive for personal gain but out of a heart that genuinely regards other people's value.

Teaching your children to say please will have a long-term, positive impact on the quality of their future personal and professional relationships. Trust me, I know.

Day 3

"No, Thank You"

*"Kindness can become its own motive.
We are made kind by being kind."*

ERIC HOFFER, AMERICAN MORAL
AND SOCIAL PHILOSOPHER

When my niece Allexa was five, I took her trick-or-treating on Halloween. All was going well until we stopped at the house of a neighbor who had only chocolate candy to offer. As the neighbor extended the bag of candy, Allexa said, "Oh, I don't like chocolate." A little embarrassed by Allexa's directness and fearful that we may have a repeat of the situation at future stops, I cautioned her (as we crept out of earshot), "Sweetheart, if someone offers you something you don't like, just say, 'No, thank you.'" She agreed and off we went.

About five houses later, we rang the doorbell and another nice neighbor pulled out a big bag of chocolate candy. Right on cue, Allexa said, "No, thank you." I felt proud and rewarded that she had learned so quickly. The neighbor, shocked that a kid would refuse any kind of treat on this special "candy night," started bombarding her with questions about why she didn't want the candy. Allexa, frustrated and not knowing what else to say, responded by yelling, "I don't like chocolate!"

Teaching your children when and *how* to say "No, thank you" is wise parenting. It not only instills politeness, it also yields other benefits, such as:

- building their confidence and self-esteem by allowing them to make choices for themselves

- building their character by teaching them to treat people and situations with kindness and respect

- teaching them that there is a right way and a wrong way to reject something

That is why it's a good idea to have the following practices in force:

- Don't allow your children to say just no; require them to say "No, thank you."

- Gently correct your children when they forget their manners.

- Compliment their saying "No, thank you" by telling them you appreciate them for doing so.

- Don't allow them to use "No, thank you" as an escape hatch to avoid things they consider unpleasant, such as eating their vegetables. Encourage them to try new foods, participate in new activities, and other things they might otherwise shy away from.

- Say "No, thank you" to them once in a while when they ask you to play a game, read their book for the sixth time, or take them to the park: "No, thank you. I'm not feeling up to that right now. We'll have to do it another time." This will be a good indoctrination in learning to accept other people's "No, thank yous."

There are times when it is perfectly appropriate and necessary for your child to just say no without the "thank you." These times include:

- being approached by a stranger and asked or told to come with them
- being touched inappropriately and asked to participate in these actions
- being pressured to participate in illegal or forbidden activities
- being told by someone in authority to do something they find uncomfortable

Child safety experts and founders of the KidSafe Foundation, Cherie Benjoseph and Sally Berenzweig, caution against the blind obedience to all authority that our parents drilled into many of us. When it comes to her ten-year-old son, Cherie explains, "We want him to be polite but *never* at the expense of his safety, and just because an adult, like a teacher or counselor, tells him to do something, if it makes him uncomfortable or confused, guess what? He doesn't have to do it! He has the right to say 'No' and he knows it."

She related an incident her son had at summer camp. The group counselor, pressed for time in getting through the activities, insisted that the boys change into their swimming trunks in an open dressing area versus the individual stalls they'd used the previous two days. Cherie's son refused, telling the counselor, "I don't want anyone to see me, and I don't want to see anyone else's privates." The counselor appealed to the director, who affirmed the boy's right to privacy.

Benjoseph and Berenzweig advise the following: "Rethink what you may be teaching them. Does your child know they have the right to say 'No' to anyone that makes them feel uncomfortable? Even an adult? Have you talked with your child about this? Do you just assume your child knows he has these rights? Or have you actually had this discussion?" [3]

Thanks, Cherie and Sally! I hope these "plain no" situations will be few and far between in your child's life.

Day 4

Greeting Others

*"A man who has friends must
himself be friendly."*
PROVERBS 18:24 NKJV

Jerry, the head of the finance department at a major
nonprofit organization, comes into the break room each
day and fails to say "good morning" to his coworkers
who have gathered there for coffee. David, one of Jerry's
more outspoken subordinates, is offended at his blatant
breach of manners and disrespect. One day, unwilling
to tolerate Jerry's conduct any longer, David decided to
take the high road by speaking first. To his dismay, Jerry
did not respond at all. David then yelled, "Jerry, I said
'Good morning!'" Only at this point did Jerry, who had
been totally distracted by his own thoughts, concede a
feeble "Good morning."

David and I concurred that extending a greeting to
a group of familiar (or even unfamiliar) people when
entering a room should be an ingrained habit. We also
concluded (perhaps a bit too judgmentally) that Jerry
had probably never received any childhood training in
relating to people. Most of the people in his department

have low regard for him due to his apparent disregard for them. It's no wonder they feel no obligation to go the extra mile when critical deadlines must be met.

Now, the case of "greetings challenged" Jesse is a little different. This teenage boy recently began dating my relative Gerry's teen daughter, Alexandria. Gerry lamented to me, "Alexandria's boyfriend is so disrespectful. When I come into the room, he doesn't say a word to me. In fact, he has *never* said anything to me at all." As I listened to his complaint, I thought, *If Jesse is always there when you enter the room, shouldn't you speak first?* (Of course, I knew that I was dealing with a stubborn father who was already biased against the young man.)

About a week after our conversation, Alexandria brought Jesse to a special dinner at our home. I greeted him warmly, teased Alexandria about how clumsily she introduced him to me (all the young folks know that I'm a stickler about such things), and went into a playful dialogue about proper greetings and introductions. He fell right into my carefully orchestrated teaching opportunity. Within minutes I had them role-playing how to introduce their moms, dads, various relatives, friends, pastors, teachers, and others. We were having a ball with it when I told them confidentially (wink) that Gerry was annoyed that Jesse had never acknowledged his presence or engaged him in conversation.

"Jesse," I asked, "why don't you speak to him?"

"I just think people should always speak to me first!" Jesse said.

I was flabbergasted. Now you can see why I'm directing this book to the parents of children in the toddler-to-twelve age range. Once kids reach the teen years, their mind-sets are often entrenched. Attempting to change them is like trying to take the sugar out of candy.

Teaching your children early on how and when to greet others will determine the first impression people have of them. Further, it will have a huge impact on the quality of their future personal and professional relationships. From the time a child learns to talk, he can be taught to say hi. Wise child raisers will reinforce this positive communication by telling a youngster, "That was really nice of you to say hi to Mr. Brown." Teach your kids that if they want friends, they must show themselves to be friendly

Caution: Once your child learns to greet people and sees how happy it makes adults to have a child initiate such contact, she may be tempted to go overboard and greet everyone she comes in contact with—including strangers. You don't want to discourage a budding Miss Congeniality or Mr. Personality; however, you must teach your children how to stay safe when away from your protection or that of a familiar, responsible adult. To this end, the National Crime Prevention Council recommends the following:

> Talk to your children about how they should handle potentially dangerous situations. One way is to teach them "No, Go, Yell, Tell." If in a dangerous situation, kids should say no, run away, yell as loud as they can, and tell a trusted adult what happened right

away. Make sure that your children know that it is okay to say no to an adult in a dangerous situation and to yell to keep themselves safe, even if they are indoors. It's good to practice this in different situations so that your children will feel confident in knowing what to do. Here are a few possible scenarios [I suggest you use these to role-play]:

- A nice-looking stranger approaches your child in the park and asks for help finding the stranger's lost dog.

- A woman who lives in your neighborhood but that the child has never spoken to invites your child into her house for a snack.

- A stranger asks if your child wants a ride home from school.

- Your child thinks he or she is being followed.

- An adult your child knows says or does something that makes him or her feel bad or uncomfortable.

- While your child is walking home from a friend's house, a car pulls over and a stranger asks for directions.[4]

The "No, Go, Yell, Tell" strategy may prove to be an over-the-top response in some situations as most strangers are nice people with no evil intentions; however, it's better to be safe than sorry. Just be careful not to teach your kids that *all* strangers are bad. After all, it just may be a good stranger who rescues him from a bad stranger!

Day 5

"Excuse Me"

"Life is short, but there is always time enough for courtesy."
RALPH WALDO EMERSON, AMERICAN
ESSAYIST AND POET

Sandra was shopping with her four-year-old son, Jordan, at a local department store when she ran into her friend Marla in the toy section. They struck up a conversation and were having a great time catching up when Jordan, holding up a red toy truck, interrupted.

"Excuse me. Excuse me, Mommy."

Sandra ignored him and continued her conversation.

"Excuse me! Excuse me! Mommy, excuse me!" he continued with increasing volume.

"Jordan, not now! Can't you see I'm talking to Miss Marla!"

"But I said 'excuse me.'"

I'm sure you've experienced or witnessed this scene countless times with young children. "Excuse me" is one of the most common phrases that kids must learn in order to develop into a polite person. Betsy Brown Braun, child development and behavior specialist and best-selling author of *Just Tell Me What to Say: Sensible Tips and Scripts for Perplexed Parents,* cautions parents to focus on an even higher purpose beyond politeness.

> We parents sabotage this lesson by teaching our kids that *excuse me* gains them entry into the conversation. We also blow it by not expecting them to wait— a little waiting at a time which grows their tolerance and their ability to delay gratification.

> Yes, we are talking about children, young children. And how hard it is for them to wait when they have something they've just got to say right now! But learning to wait and not interrupt is a lesson may be even more important than learning to say *excuse me*. It is one thing to expect your child to wait five minutes while you talk. That's a long time for a young child. It's another to teach him that when you finish your greeting, your thought, your sentence, and only then, will it be his turn.[5]

When it comes to teaching your child about interrupting you when you are working, taking a few moments for yourself, or talking with someone else, you will find it useful to do the following.

Expect to be interrupted. Young children don't realize or understand what it is to interrupt. They just know they need or want your attention and that, for the most part, you have met their previous needs in a timely and satisfactory manner. They see no reason to think now will be any different.

Teach them to give you a specific signal when they want

or need to speak to you. Some parents teach their toddlers and preschoolers to touch their leg or take hold of their hand before speaking. In doing so, you can make eye contact with them and either ask them to wait or excuse yourself from whatever you are doing and let them speak.

As your toddlers morph into preschoolers, you can *teach them to use situational expressions* ("May I talk to you?" or "I need you"), depending on the circumstances. For example, if your preschooler comes rushing in saying, "I need you," you will know there is a situation (urgent request to use the restroom, potential danger, etc.) that demands your immediate attention because you have taught them to use that phrase only for such times.

Set guidelines. Once your children reach school age, they should know full well what is and isn't appropriate when it comes to interrupting you. Once those guidelines are set, insist your children comply with them.

When setting guidelines for interrupting, here are a few suggestions that have proven to be effective:

- Post a "Do Not Disturb" sign when you are enjoying some quiet time or intimate time with your spouse. Explain to your kids what circumstances will allow them to knock on the door to interrupt (injury, choking, etc.).
- When interacting with your kids, extend the same courtesy to them unless they are in an unacceptable situation.
- Teach your children to use their reasoning and

problem-solving skills to cut back on their need (or assumed need) to interrupt you so that you might solve their problems.

Teaching your children *when* to interrupt, *when not* to interrupt, and *how* to interrupt will best be learned when it's modeled by you. If they see you interrupting your spouse, know that you have sent a mixed message.

I was counseling a couple once and asked them to take turns giving their perspective on the problem. The woman spoke first at great length. However, when it was the husband's turn, she continually interrupted him with comments about what he had said. She had absolutely no experience in waiting her turn to talk. Could it be that she was never taught this skill as a child?

Beyond interrupting, your kids need to learn to say "excuse me" at other times, such as when they:

- belch or accidentally pass gas
- unintentionally slurp the last of their drink with a straw
- inadvertently step on someone's foot or bump into them
- sneeze or yawn (Be sure to teach them to cover their mouth.)
- need to get someone's attention
- need someone to repeat something ("Excuse me?")

- press through a crowd of people
- reach across someone (For example, reaching to press an elevator button. Better to request the person nearest the control panel to press the button for your floor.)

Even if you are not a parent but are a part of a child's "influencer village," be diligent in instilling these guidelines. This will be an investment that will pay big social returns.

Day 6

"Sorry!" Versus Apologizing

"Never ruin an apology with an excuse."
BENJAMIN FRANKLIN

Samantha was sorry she got caught cheating on a test, but was too embarrassed and too proud to apologize to the rest of the class who had to take the test over.

Maggie never dreamed not inviting Abigail to her party would cause such a problem. It wasn't that she didn't like Abigail—they just didn't have anything in common. But when some of the girls at the party started talking about Abigail and posting untrue things about her on social network sites, Maggie felt terrible. She hadn't done anything wrong personally, but it happened at her party, so she felt responsible. Maggie went to Abigail and her mom and apologized. She said she knew what was said wasn't true and that she wished she had done more to stop the other girls.

Five-year-old Olivia was upset that Ann had tattled on her for making the finger-painting mess on the kitchen table. To retaliate, Olivia broke Ann's new doll that crawled and giggled. Ann was devastated! She'd gotten the doll for Christmas only a week before and now it was ruined. Olivia was sent to her room to think about what she had done and what she thought should be done as a result of her actions. Being the typical five-year-old, not much thinking went on until Ann said to her, "You didn't just break my doll. You made me sad and broke my heart. It's like undoing Christmas." Ann's words caused Olivia to feel extremely remorseful. She apologized and said she was very sorry. Further, she offered to use her piggy-bank savings to help buy Ann another doll. They grew up to be as close as two sisters can be.

Apologizing is acknowledging your hurtful action ("I apologize for eating your candy bar without getting your permission"); it's the reason you need to feel sorry. Being sorry is an expression of your regret and remorse for such action. When you say "I'm sorry," you focus on the hurt or inconvenience you caused the other person.

Many parents unwisely insist their children say sorry, which they are often willing to do when further conse-quences are threatened. But simply saying sorry is an incomplete apology. Here are the essentials elements of a complete apology based on Psalm 51—the passage King David wrote to God after he slept with Bathsheba and had her husband killed to hide the resulting pregnancy (2 Samuel 11).

- Acknowledge the specific offense. ("I apologize for breaking the vase.")
- Admit remorse. ("I'm so sorry. I feel really bad

about it because I know how much it meant to
you.")

- Accept full responsibility for your actions. ("I
take responsibility for my actions. I shouldn't
have been running through the house.") Don't
make excuses or blame anyone else—especially
the victim. ("I was running because my brother
was chasing me." "You shouldn't have placed the
vase in such a bad spot.")

- Ask for forgiveness. ("Please forgive me.")

- Assure a change in future behavior. ("It won't
happen again. I promise not to run in the house
and to be careful to watch where I'm going.")

- Attempt to make amends where possible. ("I'm
willing to save from my allowance until I get
enough money to replace the vase.")

Adults and kids can apply this model to almost any
offense. Darla Noble, a seasoned parent and grand-
mother who has written numerous articles and resources
on parenting and family life, explained to me how she's
put similar principles into play during her parenting
experience.

> We never forced our four children to say, "I'm
> sorry." To have forced them to say something
> they didn't mean would have been useless and
> empty. Instead, we put them in a position of see-
> ing or experiencing the result of what they had
> said or done. They had to listen to their sibling

cry or express their anger or hurt. They had to relinquish their toy or treat to the sibling they had mistreated. They had to clean and bandage the cut or scrape they caused. Our intentions were for them to personally experience remorse and regret rather than simply saying "I'm sorry."

So, parent, if you have noticed that your child is not quick to apologize when he hurts or offends others, try these strategies:

- Make apologizing part of your personal habits. No child will miss the valuable lesson to be learned when a parent apologizes for hurting his feelings, overreacting, or being insensitive. ("Johnnie, I apologize for not letting you explain the full story of how the window got broken. Please forgive me.")

- Teach the offended child to express his feelings to the offender. ("I felt embarrassed when you poked fun of my hair in front of your friends." "I felt sad when you broke my doll.")

- Talk to your children regularly about how our words and actions affect others and the responsibility we have to treat people in a kind and positive way.

Teaching your children to deliver an effective and timely apology is an important lesson that will serve them well throughout their lives. It can save them from emotional turmoil and equip them with people skills needed to make them topnotch spouses, parents, friends, neighbors, employers, employees, and servants of God. Raising sympathetic and compassionate children who are willing and capable of being held accountable for their actions is a gift you give to the world.

Day 7

Addressing Adults

*"Stand up in the presence of the elderly,
and show respect for the aged."*

LEVITICUS 19:32

Here's how Junie in Barbara Park's hilarious Junie B. Jones series of children's books describes her kindergarten teacher: "Her name is Mrs. She has another name, too, but I just like Mrs. and that's all." Junie may leave off the last name of her teacher, but at least she has the proper way of addressing an adult down pat.

When it comes to teaching your children how to properly address the adults in their lives, there are no clear-cut definitions of what is always appropriate and inappropriate. Of course, there are the givens (or so one would think), such as Grammy and Papa or whatever substitute names the adult prefers. There used to be (and still should be) others that fall into this category: teachers, coaches, the parents of your kids' friends, and even aunts and uncles.

But let's face it, times have changed. While it is never wrong or inappropriate to teach and expect your children to address their elders respectfully, there are instances where adults do not desire titles such as Mr. or Mrs. Let's look at several examples that show both sides of the issue:

- A certain Christian youth camp is staffed by volunteers with a passion for youth ministry. They spend considerable time with the children and teens who attend the camp each summer and have developed close, trusting relationships with the kids. Because of this, the staff prefers the kids to call them by their first names. "It would make me uncomfortable for them to do otherwise," one staff member said. "I would feel that I didn't have the trust of the kids," said another.

- Mary asserts, "I don't care how old I am, I will never address my aunts and uncles in any other way *but* Aunt So-and-So or Uncle So-and-So. That's how I was brought up. It shows that I respect their place in the family. To call them simply by their first names would be like saying I didn't love them as much."

- Many coaches prefer to be called Coach (First Name) rather than Miss or Mr. By using the title Coach, the respect for authority is still present, but there is also a trust or camaraderie initiated by using a first name.

- Laura Rader has been the director of a church daycare center for nearly twenty years. She's always asked the children to call her Miss Laura

instead of Miss Rader. Even the parents call
her Miss Laura. That's just how she wants to be
addressed.

Each of these situations makes a solid case that most
parents would find no fault with. But that still doesn't
answer the question of how to know whom to address
formally versus informally. Since it often boils down to
individual preference, try the following as general guidelines for your child to follow:

- Address any person in authority by their title as
  a sign of respect for both the person and their
  position. This includes pastors (Pastor _____),
  police officers (Officer _____), and teachers
  (Mrs./Miss/Mr. _____).

- Address adult family members by the appropriate title and their name. Aunt _____, Uncle
  _____, Cousin _____, and so on.

- Address nonrelated adults as Mr./Mrs./Miss
  (Last Name) or Mr./Mrs./Miss (First Name). If
  in doubt, ask them how they would like to be
  addressed.

- Refer to friends' parents as Mr. or Mrs. (Last
  Name). Exceptions to this rule should occur
  only if the adult in question asks to be called
  by their first name. Even so, if you feel strongly
  about not allowing your children to do this,
  gently say so.

When it comes to teaching your children how and

why they should address the adults in their lives in certain ways, it is important to convey that these titles are more than just words. Your children need to know that such titles acknowledge their understanding of respect and authority, as well as honor the adult's position.

As a parent, remember to extend a bit of grace to your children when they don't get it right. Politely remind them of your expectations and guidelines. Your instructions to your children will carry more weight if you also adhere to the same standards in certain situations. For instance, it is completely realistic for your children to expect you to address or refer to your friends, their teacher, or the next-door neighbors as Mr./Mrs./Miss _____ (when children are present) rather than by their first names.

As an aunt, I take the liberty to correct my nieces and nephews if they do not address me properly—although it rarely happens. Several years ago, however, I was relating an incident to my ten-year-old-niece, and she said, "Girl, you are lying!" I was flabbergasted at her use of such familiar language with me. I gently told her that addressing me that way was unacceptable. I said, "Listen, Sweetheart, I'm not your friend or your peer. I'm your aunt. You're going to have to address me as Aunt Deborah." She knew I was not joking and she complied. We haven't had a problem with this issue since.

So I challenge aunts and uncles and other kinfolk to remember that "it takes a village to raise a child." Be sure to do your part in keeping your young relatives on the respect track.

Day 8

Using the Indoor Voice

"One man's rights end where another's begin."
AUTHOR UNKNOWN

The Sunday evening Bible fellowship was in full swing at the small rural church. The pastor was starting a new study on the New Testament book of James. He began by giving a brief introduction to the book—who wrote it, when it was written, the overall theme, and so on. About thirty people were in attendance, including a young couple with their four children. Emma, the youngest, sat quietly on the pew playing with her doll. When the pastor said that James was the brother of Jesus, Emma popped up out of her seat and said loudly, "Preacher Dave, I didn't know Jesus had a brother! That's cool!" Preacher Dave said, "Yep, He sure did," and went right on with the Bible lesson (after the laughter subsided).

Around the time your children reach the age of three, they develop a problem with volume control—they don't have any. They know how to talk only one way— L-O-U-D! Once they start school, they usually grasp the concept of using their "indoor voice" in the classroom, at the dinner table, and hopefully in public places.

Failure to use their indoor voice doesn't always work out so well for toddlers or their parents. The lack of volume control has been known to embarrass parents and anger those subjected to their innocent indiscretions. That's why parents must take the time to teach small children to speak quietly

- inside the house (thus the designation *indoor voice*)
- in church, restaurants, on airplanes, and other public places
- in close proximity to the person they are speaking to

When teaching children to use their indoor voice, most parents say they have the most success when they:

Give their child their full attention when he is talking lest he think that talking louder will make them focus on him.

Demonstrate the difference between an indoor and an outdoor voice. Little children don't deliberately yell to get on your nerves or because they think they need to. Their lack of volume control is usually from their excitement over what they have to say.

Refuse to answer questions or address needs that are spoken too loudly (unless there's a real emergency). These parents simply and quietly tell their kids they will answer them when they speak in their indoor voice. Please note that if your child doesn't grasp the concept of using an indoor voice, you may need to have his hearing evaluated to rule out the possibility of auditory problems.

When Chicago restaurant owner Dan McCauley became fed up with loud kids, he posted a sign on his front door: "Children of all ages have to behave and use their indoor voices." Several parents took offense and concluded that their kids were not welcome in his establishment. They missed the point entirely. Please don't be the type of parent who is oblivious to your child's noise pollution and the damper that it can put on other people's dining experience. One of my favorite grade-school teachers used to say, "One man's rights end where another man's rights begin." Other people have a right to pleasant dining without tolerating noisy kids.

Once you make it through those early years and your child learns the value of speaking quietly in certain environments, don't think you can breathe a sigh of relief just yet. As your children enter puberty, they tend to revert to being loud and out of control. With girls, it's the high-pitched squealing, giggling, and screaming. With boys, it takes the form of hollering, rousting around, and boasting and bragging about muscles, athletic accomplishments, and so forth.

You may be tempted to give them a dose of their own medicine by *yelling* at them (versus *asking*) to take out the trash, get their homework done, or come to the dinner table. Some parents say this works in their households. However, know that this trains your children that yelling is the standard for getting results. A better way is to tell your children that you cannot answer them when they speak to you so loudly because it is difficult for you to concentrate on the conversation. When they get the message that they won't be heard until they lower their volume, you can bet it won't take long. I'm a big proponent of boundaries with consequences.

When it comes to your tweens and teens, let their lack of volume control go once in a while. So they giggle and squeal. So they let out a few high-pitched screams of excitement or shock over who likes whom or what happened in English class. So the boys get a bit rowdy as they try to outdo each other's stories and think that the louder they tell it the better it is. One experienced mom had this to say:

> Take it from a mom whose children are grown and out on their own. Teaching your kids to use their indoor voice may not always come easily, and it may seem you'll never have a quiet and peaceful household, but in only a few blinks of an eye, it's quiet. Very quiet.

Day 9

Admitting Mistakes, Wrongdoing, and Failings

*"People who conceal their sins will not prosper,
but if they confess and turn from them,
they will receive mercy."*

PROVERBS 28:13

Seth was the apple of his parents' eye. He was handsome, made good grades, and could play baseball like nobody's business. He was only a sophomore in high school when the scouts started looking at him. The family was wealthy and well-known around town, and Seth fully embraced the idea of taking over the family business someday. He was every parent's dream child. Unfortunately, the dream became a nightmare one night when, driving drunk, he hit a young mother who had gone out for a run while her husband watched their new baby.

Not willing to admit their son's grave mistake, Seth's parents argued that the young woman wasn't dressed appropriately for jogging at dusk. It didn't seem to matter to them that their son was seventeen (drinking illegally), driving drunk, and that his car had jumped the curb and crashed into the victim—who was wearing a bright orange shirt!

Even Seth's baseball coach came to his defense. He reportedly told someone that the whole thing was being blown out of proportion—boys will be boys, you know. Tell that to the mother who had two broken legs and internal bleeding.

Seth had been led to believe his entire life that someone or something else was always to blame for his behavior. Thankfully, that all changed with the accident. Justice was served, and Seth will forever remember that he was at fault and that he was made to take responsibility for his mistakes.

Owning up to our mistakes is one of the hardest things we do. It's also one of the hardest things to teach your children to do. It's a lot like teaching them to tell the truth. We humans seem to have this instinct to protect ourselves by putting up a shield of blamelessness. "I didn't do that." "I'm not the one who messed that up." We just have a hard time admitting our faults. But why?

Fear of being rejected is one of the major reasons children deny responsibility for their mistakes. They are so afraid of being rejected by you…by their coach…by their teacher. Society puts so much emphasis on being the best, looking the best, and getting ahead. A child's fear of being rejected because of a mistake comes also from the fact that they see it in action all the time. Kids on the soccer team quit talking to the player who continually misses the goal. Girls who make the mistake of showing up at school wearing the "wrong" thing are ostracized. Kids who don't side with the "right" parent in the divorce suddenly don't see Mom or Dad very often.

Low self-esteem is another reason kids refuse to admit their mistakes. This ties in to the fear of rejection, but it also encompasses fear of failing. Children with low self-esteem see mistakes as personal failures rather than the life-lessons they are.

Lack of a role model. Plenty of children can't or won't admit their mistakes because their parents don't admit theirs. Children who live in such households live under the false assumption that their family is blameless and that it is always someone else's fault.

Parents do a great disservice to their children when they don't allow them to mess up. Teach your children that it's okay to make mistakes. Teach them that making mistakes doesn't make them less of a person, but rather can make them wiser, stronger, and more knowledgeable.

After experiment number 678, Thomas Edison still didn't know how to make a lightbulb, but he knew 678 ways how not to make one. So teach your children that:

Mistakes are part of life. No one gets almost anything right the first time. So what?

Mistakes won't make you love them less. Children want to please you and make you proud of them. They crave your acceptance. You must let them know by your words, your actions, and your attitude that your love for them is unconditional—that mistakes or the lack thereof don't have anything to do with how much you love them.

Mistakes build character. When we make mistakes, we put ourselves in the position of being humbled.

Humility usually leads to compassion, which leads to reaching out to others.

Mistakes don't define you. Your children need to be taught that we can and should learn from our mistakes rather than letting them hold us hostage. Impress upon your children that just because they failed a math test doesn't make them a failure in math. They need to understand that just because they didn't follow the directions and made a mistake that cost them their entry in the science fair doesn't mean they are incompetent. Instead, you need to be compassionate and encouraging while holding them accountable so that they don't end up like Seth the under-aged drunk driver. In doing so, your children will learn that their mistakes don't need to define them, but should help determine their direction.

Many famous people and corporations made (and continue to make) mistakes. Coke's big mistake in trying to change the flavor of its famous soft drink didn't ruin them. They just went back to what had worked before. Henry Ford's Edsel was a disaster, but that mistake didn't stop him from producing automobiles, including the iconic Mustang.

Mistakes are inevitable but not insurmountable. Instill this truth into your kids.

Day 10

Communicating with People Who Are Different

"For you are all one in Christ Jesus."
GALATIANS 3:28

Opal is different. She obviously has learning disabilities. She also wears clothes that are tattered and much too big for her. She has long, unkempt hair, crooked teeth, and talks with a lisp. She is also one of the best rope jumpers in the school.

Allan is in a wheelchair. His arms and legs don't work. Sometimes the kids can see his urine in a bag when he wears shorts. He is funny and can sing really well.

Jerome is the only black kid in the entire elementary school in the elite, predominantly white suburb. He is quite shy but very smart; he always makes the honor roll. Most of the time, he eats lunch alone in the school cafeteria since the other kids are not quite sure what to say to him.

Inevitably, your children will discover that some of the kids in your neighborhood or at their school are different from them. Not knowing how to deal with these differences may cause them to make fun of or avoid them. Children do this because they feel uncomfortable and unfamiliar with the situation. However, just as you teach your kids how to greet and interact with other children and adults, it is just as important to teach them through *exposure* and *empathy* how to communicate effectively with those who are different.

Exposure

Hoping to show a way for nondisabled children to overcome the discomfort or anxiety of interacting with disabled children, doctoral candidate Megan MacMillan authored a study of over fifteen hundred children between the ages of seven and sixteen at the University of Exeter Medical School in the United Kingdom. The study concluded that "increased exposure to people whose range of abilities is more limited than others' builds prolonged comfort, not only with the specific disability, but also with encountering diversity more broadly later in life." [6]

Here are some ways that some parents suggest you expose your children to other kids and adults who are different:

- Attend ethnic festivals.
- Volunteer at nursing homes and homes for the disabled.
- Involve your children in organizations that don't have social and economic boundaries (such as Girl Scouts and 4-H Club).
- Be the self-appointed ambassador to your neighborhood. Welcome new families and offer to show them around town. Invite them to your

home for a meal. Host a "meet and greet" for their children with your children and their friends.

- Encourage your children to befriend those who are different.

Empathy

The MacMillan study went on to conclude, "Simply observing others interacting with disabled children or being aware that others are friends with them can improve attitudes. This 'indirect contact' reduces anxiety and increases empathy towards disabled people." [7]

Here are a few fundamental ideas that you should impress upon your children to help them become empathetic to those who are different.

Everyone is different in some way—including your children. Talk to your kids about how they would like to be treated if they were physically handicapped or different in any way from the majority of their classmates or playmates. Ask what they would or would not want other kids to say to them or about them. Most children will easily become empathetic. This is a good time to admonish them that you will not tolerate name-calling and teasing a person who is different.

A person's difference is just one aspect of his life. Therefore, your kid should not view a disabled person through just one lens ("the blind boy," "the girl in the wheelchair"). Reiterate that the disabled person wants the same thing as your child: to be accepted and included.

Mephibosheth became crippled at the age of five when his nurse dropped him. She was fleeing with him from the palace after hearing that King Saul (Mephibosheth's grandfather) and Jonathan (his father) had been killed in battle (2 Samuel 4:4). Years later when King David took the throne, he honored his oath to his friend Jonathan and insisted that Mephibosheth dine at his table. "And Mephibosheth, who was crippled in both feet, lived in Jerusalem and ate regularly at the king's table" (2 Samuel 9:13). Imagine how validating that must have been for him to sit at the king's table each day as an equal with David's children. I believe this is a model for how to treat people who are different—with complete acceptance.

Stress to your kids that those with physical disabilities are impaired only in the area of their disability. Do not assume that they are also *mentally* impaired. Teach your kids to resist speaking to them in an overly sympathetic "I-feel-so-sorry-for-you" or condescending tone.

By the same token, don't discourage them from being direct and asking questions about the disability during a one-on-one (never a group) encounter with the disabled person. *Example:* "What happened to cause you to be in the wheelchair?" Listen, it's okay to address the disability with an attitude of concern and a desire to understand. Most of the time, it's looming like an elephant in the room anyway. Usually the adults are the ones who are uncomfortable and shy away from disabled adults in a social situation—because no one taught them this lesson.

Teach your children that we all have in common the fact that we are all precious in God's sight. That's the most important thing you need to make sure they know.

Day 11

Speaking Up

"Learn to do good.
Seek justice.
Help the oppressed."
ISAIAH 1:17

One of the biggest predictors of the quality of your child's present and future relationships is how well he learns to use his voice to express how he feels about the activities and behaviors within his circle of interaction. Lisa M. Schab, licensed clinical social worker and author of *Cool, Calm, and Confident: A Workbook to Help Kids Learn Assertiveness Skills*, says that assertiveness is the "healthiest style of communication. Assertiveness involves recognizing and standing up for our own rights, while at the same time recognizing and respecting the rights of others." [8]

As I see it, there are three critical areas where children must be taught to speak up.

Personal religious beliefs. In chapter 2, we met Daniel and the group of young Israelite men who were taken captive to Babylon. They had to go through a period of nourishment and training to serve in King

Nebuchadnezzar's court. Because of his strong conviction about not eating non-kosher foods, Daniel spoke up and asked that he and his three friends be allowed to follow a vegetarian diet. As a result, they were better nourished than all the ones who followed the king's eating plan. He stood for his beliefs.

We've all heard the adage that "if you don't stand for something, you'll fall for anything." All children need a solid belief system to keep them anchored lest they just go with the tide of whatever comes along. Parents do their children a great disservice when they do not give them early on a foundation of faith, morals, and core principles. Many struggle throughout adulthood because they don't have the sure footing of strong beliefs. Whoever thought it was a good idea to let them wait until they're grown and decide for themselves?

Wise parents teach their kids how to stand up for their beliefs and express them in an effective way. Of course, teaching your children to *speak up* for what is right begins with living the example of what's right. If you don't model a strong commitment to what you say you believe, how are your children going to have the confidence and courage to speak out instead of keeping quiet for fear of being ridiculed? Learning to say, "This is what I believe," without being obnoxious or overbearing, comes first by observing a great example at home.

Harm, threats, or injustices to themselves or to others. Instill in your children the words to say when they feel fearful or threatened by an adult or another child. As soon as they learn to speak, drill into them what an inappropriate touch is. Explain that there is a "good touch" and a "bad touch." Demonstrate what each looks like. For example, a quick hug or a handshake is a good touch; any contact with their private parts is a bad touch. Admonish your kids to tell you promptly if they receive a bad touch. "Mom, my [teacher/uncle/*anybody*] gave me a bad touch today."

Teach your kids to quietly report to a person in authority any time they see someone being bullied, ridiculed, or treated unfairly or any activities that are a threat to the common good. Currently, the US Department of Homeland Security is running a "If You See Something, Say Something" public awareness campaign in which people are admonished to report any activity where terrorism might be suspected. This would be a good campaign to adopt for your children as it relates to any activity where a group of people could be harmed, such as a kid with a weapon or someone playing with fire.

Children also need to know that there is a right way and a wrong way to stand up for what is right. It is critical that you teach them to be respectful of what other people believe and their right to believe it. There is never a need for name-calling, hitting, or other misbehaving to defend your beliefs.

Other times to speak up. In addition to the circumstances above, children should be encouraged to speak up when they

- have a solution to a problem
- have an idea or opinion they wish to express

- want to give someone else recognition for good deeds he has done

Finally, there are also times when it's best for children *not* to speak up. No, that doesn't mean you are to encourage them to wimp out or compromise their values. Instead, you are teaching them wisdom. Thus, a wise parent teaches their child it is best to keep quiet if speaking up will

- endanger his life or well-being
- expose another person to danger
- only make the situation worse

Teaching your children to be assertive and to speak up increases their self-esteem. In turn, good self-esteem is one of the strongest safeguards against a child becoming a bully or being bullied. Again, I encourage you to role-play with your child about how to respond to various situations where speaking up is the best solution. The overriding question should always be: "Will my speaking up help the situation or bring harm?"

By implementing the recommendations above, you will help your child develop into a strong, assertive, expressive, empowered, and respected adult.

Day 12

Handling Secrets

*"A time to keep silence,
And a time to speak."*
ECCLESIASTES 3:7 NKJV

My four-year-old niece decided to watch me put on makeup and do my hair as I dressed to go to a family function. To save time, I decided to wear a wig. I said to her, "Now Shawnda, nobody knows this is a wig, so don't say anything when we get to the party." She promised to keep my secret. As soon as we walked in the door, she ran to her mother and blurted (not in her indoor voice), "Auntie Deborah is wearing a wig!"

Children are infamous for letting the cat out of the bag. Here are just a few more examples:

- "We're staying at Aunt Margaret's house because we're getting poor and my mom doesn't have a job right now."—five-year-old Sam

- "My dad says your dad is a geek. What's a geek?"—seven-year-old Shawn

- "My mom says new math is what you're getting

paid for teaching so you should have to be the one to help me."—eight-year-old Tessa

Most of these verbal indiscretions are innocent. Some are the result of the parents not watching what they say around their kids. But how do you teach your children to filter the difference between what's meant to be kept private and what isn't? At what stage should you teach them?

Well, toddlers and preschoolers can't keep secrets. They don't even know what a secret is. They are naïve and there is no gray area so they call 'em as they see 'em.

School-aged children gradually learn what is acceptable for sharing and what isn't as long as you've taken the time to teach them the difference between honest and rude, safe and confidential, and tactful and tacky.

(*Caution*: It's important to teach your children that if anyone asks them to keep a secret from you, they should tell you immediately—even if the requester threatens to kill parents or siblings. Let your children know that the person is bluffing. Sadly, some parents are guilty of using the secret-keeping ploy to hide sexual and physical abuse in the home.)

Keeping their lips zipped can be too much to expect from a child, and expecting too much from your children is never a good idea. Let's look at how to help your children know what they should and shouldn't *say* as well as what you should and shouldn't *tell* them.

- When you don't want them to blab about a certain matter, preface what you say with "This is something we aren't ready for anyone to know who does not live here." Or say, "I'm asking you to not tell anyone this. This is a family matter."

- Do tell children of school age if your family is going to be relocating. It's important that you prepare them for this major life-event. Asking them to keep it quiet until you are ready to share is acceptable.

- If you choose to tell your children that Santa Claus, the tooth fairy, and the Easter bunny are only make-believe "friends," do tell them that they aren't to share your family's views. You don't have the right to ruin another child's fantasy.

- Don't share the details of household financial woes with your children. They don't need to worry—and they will—even though they don't fully understand what's happening. Plus, they might say something you don't want made public.

- Do explain that family arguments and issues such as a sibling's misbehavior may need to be discussed as a family but don't need to leave the walls of your house.

- Don't allow your children to discuss the details of a divorce or custody agreement with inquisitive grandparents, relatives, or strangers. Your children need to know what's going to be taking place in your lives, but the general public and prying relatives do not.

- Do tell your children that they should always come to you if someone tells them something that will lead to illegal or unsafe activity or consequences.

- Do tell your children that it is *always* best to tell you or someone they trust when they see unsafe or illegal activity.

- Do tell children that keeping quiet about surprise parties and gifts you are giving to a family member or friend are good secrets that should be kept.

- Admonish your children to tell you if someone has given them a gift and told them not to tell.

When teaching your children the how and what of knowing when to speak up and when to keep quiet, you also need to explain why some things are meant to be shared and some things are not. Encourage them to evaluate the situation by asking themselves:

- Have my parents asked me to keep the information in the family?

- Will this information help someone by bringing him to safety or keeping him from harm?

- Is keeping quiet assisting someone illegally?

- Who is asking…and why? Can they help? Are they trustworthy?

- Is this something that goes against our family values?

- Will saying something hurt someone's feelings or embarrass them?

- Will saying something get someone in trouble, yet save them from danger?

- What benefits are there to me in saying something?

By teaching your children how to evaluate what information to offer up and what not to, you will be building trust with your child, giving them valuable social and survival skills, and saving yourself lots of red-faced moments.

Day 13

Giving and Accepting Compliments

*"So encourage each other and build each
other up, just as you are already doing."*

1 Thessalonians 5:11

"Auntie Deborah, look at me!" five-year-old Taylor yelled as she pumped herself higher than normal on the park swing. "No, look at *me*!" screamed her little brother as he did a complicated flip on the grass. I'd volunteered to babysit our young pastor's energetic kids for the afternoon, and boy was I glad for the nearby park. I knew from my many playdates with kids that they were not shouting for me to merely look at them; they wanted me to applaud their efforts. I didn't disappoint them.

Giving Compliments

Compliments are encouraging and motivating. They make people feel good about themselves. Learning to give and receive compliments is an important aspect of developing character and good people skills. When teaching your children why and when to compliment others, they will easily embrace the idea of wanting to make someone feel good. To this end, your instructions to them might include a script that goes like this: "It makes you feel good when someone notices your new shoes or how well you ride your bike, doesn't it? It's nice for you to make other people feel good too by telling them what a great job they're doing or how nice they look."

Teaching your children to be generous with their accolades and to give honest compliments will help them develop an appreciation for the skills and talents of others. They can learn early on to applaud another person's accomplishments instead of being self-centered, envious, or competitive. They can reject the faulty thinking that an accolade for someone else—especially a sibling—is a strike against them.

Oh, the family strife that could be avoided if parents encouraged their children to find something to praise or admire about their siblings. Imagine a game in which the winner is the child who gives the highest number of sincere praises to his brother or sister. Even outside the home, you can teach your children to look for things to admire in their classmates, friends, and teachers—and to tell them so.

Don't expect your children to always feel like complimenting others. They are still growing and maturing emotionally. So when your twelve-year-old daughter's best friend gets the same jacket she really, really hoped you'd buy her, it's only natural for her to not want to compliment her on how great she looks wearing it.

However, if you teach her to press past those feelings, she will learn a great lesson in humility and a powerful way to stop envy in its tracks.

Caution: Teach your kids that their compliments are to be sincere and without any intent to manipulate or gain more friends. Friends will be a natural outcome because people like to be with people who make them feel good about themselves. But when compliments are reduced to selfish motives, then your kid's integrity is questioned.

Of course, a child's ability to give compliments is nurtured by a healthy self-esteem. When your children know they have your unconditional love and that you are proud of them "just because," they won't feel threatened by the accomplishments and recognition others receive. Feeling secure leaves more room for recognizing the good in other people and being happy for their good fortune. Compliments such as the following should be readily expressed at home:

"You look nice."

"Wow. You really made your bed neatly."

"That pop fly you caught was amazing."

"I like your (whatever)."

"That was nice of you to share your toys."

Notice that each compliment is specific enough for the child to know exactly what behavior you are praising and appreciating. However, most child experts agree that it is more beneficial to praise your child's *efforts* than their *results*. General extreme praise, such as "You are the smartest kid in the world," is detrimental. In fact, six studies showed that praise for a kid's intelligence had a more negative impact on motivation than praise for effort. Fifth graders praised for intelligence were found to care more about performance than learning. After a failure, the performers also displayed less task enjoyment than children praised for effort.[9]

A friend tells the story of how her mother-in-law had always built up my friend's husband, calling him her "one-hundred-million-dollar gold piece." Imagine starting a relationship with someone whose ego has been so grossly massaged. Fortunately, they worked through the issues this exaggerated praise created.

You must be careful not to give your kids a false sense of accomplishment. Complimenting a child for her progress on the flute when it's clearly *not* going well isn't doing her any favors. It sets her up for rejection and disappointment when the stark reality hits her that she is mediocre at best. It is wiser to say, "I really admire your determination to play the flute. Keep at it. Hard work pays off." Consider that it may be time to ask for godly wisdom on how to redirect her efforts. Building a false sense of security in your child is too big a risk to her future development and relationships.

Even when kids are excellent, you must be careful to compliment them in a way that keeps their accomplishments in perspective lest you turn them into a performance junkie who lives for praise and recognition. Later in life, such kids often grow up to be unhappy, unfulfilled workaholics and sore losers.

Accepting Compliments

When the apostle Paul admonished the Christians in Thessalonica to "encourage each other and to build each other up" (1 Thessalonians 5:11), he clearly meant for compliments and praises to flow both ways. Therefore, your kids need to know how to *receive* compliments and accolades. Teach them that it's okay to acknowledge a compliment by simply saying "Thank you" or "I enjoy playing (a certain instrument, sport)" or "It's great to know someone noticed." The typical "Oh, it's nothing" response is false modesty. It also refutes the judgment of the one giving the compliment.

God made us unique and special in different ways. It's perfectly okay to know that. Just remind your kids that apart from God, they can do absolutely nothing. Jesus said, "I am the vine, you are the branches. He who abides in Me, and I in him, bears much fruit; for without Me you can do nothing" (John 15:5 NKJV). Therefore, they must give all the credit and honor for their accomplishments to God—in their hearts. No need for them to respond to a compliment by saying, "Oh, it wasn't me; it was the Lord." They just need to *remember* that.

Keeping Family Matters Private

"What happens at home stays at home!"
EVERY PARENT

Art Linkletter was a master at interviewing children. He created the long-running TV show *Art Linkletter's House Party,* which included a segment called "Kids Say the Darndest Things." Linkletter would interview young kids, and their responses would usually be cute, unpredictable, and humorous. Once he asked a grammar-school boy what his father did for a living. The boy replied in a very animated way,

> "My dad's a cop! He catches crooks and burglars and spread-eagles 'em and put cuffs on 'em and takes 'em down to the station and puts 'em in the slammer." "Wow," Art replied, "I bet your mother gets worried about his work, doesn't she?" "Heck no!" the youth assured Art. "He brings her lots of watches and rings and jewelry." [10]

Leave it to a youngster to shine the spotlight on the skeletons in the family closet.

To minimize embarrassing moments, parents must be vigilant in guarding the things they disclose in the presence of their kids. Don't think that you can talk with your best friend about your "dreadful" mother-in-law or the "nasty" neighbor next door, while your darling little sponge sits there taking it all in. At the slightest "squeeze" or opportunity, anything she had absorbed is likely to come out.

TMI is a popular acronym today. It stands for Too Much Information. When someone begins to indiscreetly reveal matters that should be kept private, the listener exclaims (usually lightheartedly) "TMI!" Well, parents, you'll have to become more conscious of TMI boundaries with your kids. It really is critical to begin teaching them the importance of privacy at an early age by letting your kids know that what happens in your household stays in your household.

Let's look at what some wise parents said about what family business is appropriate to share with children at their various stages of development.

Preschooler Through Age Six

You don't tell a preschooler *anything* you don't want shared. It's too confusing to them. On one hand you tell them not to keep bad secrets from you, and then on the other hand you tell them to keep family secrets. The rule on this is really quite simple: don't tell them anything that you are not comfortable with someone else finding out. Children are innocent and have no insecurities or concerns about protecting their image—or yours. I love how they can easily talk to outsiders about the most delicate family matters. (Frankly, I think that if parents were sometimes a bit more transparent with others about certain problems, they would find hope and help in surprising places.)

According to my informal "parent poll," the things you *should* share with your preschooler and early school-aged children include:

- that he or she is adopted (Other people will likely know this, so you'll surely want to tell him or her before someone else does.)

- the expected arrival of a new baby

- that the family is moving (It's traumatic at this age, so be gentle, positive, and encouraging no matter how you feel about the situation.)

- news of the death of a family member

- news of a marital separation, divorce, or upcoming military deployment

The things you should *not* share or discuss in the presence of children in this age range include:

- household financial woes (Six-year-old Mary innocently told her teacher that their family didn't have to pay money for food any more since her dad lost his job. Now they pay with "pieces of paper" [food stamps].)

- troubles of extended family members
- gossip or news about friends, neighbors, or other relatives
- marital disagreements

Ages Seven to Twelve

The above guidelines also apply to children in this age group, although they can handle a few more details. For example, while you may tell them the family is moving or that there is going to be an adjustment in the family's lifestyle, it is not necessary for them to know how much debt you have or that you owe more on your mortgage than the house is worth.

If you and your spouse are separating or divorcing, your bitterness about an affair or the fact your ex is marrying someone you do not like shouldn't be interjected into the conversation. You'll just be planting the seeds for angry, confused kids. Go for harmony and ask God for the grace to take the high road in relational matters.

If someone close to them is critically or terminally ill, you'll want them to know that "Grandma has lived a full life" or "Aunt Sarah is very ill." Answer their questions openly and honestly, but don't be too graphic or too detailed. Also, be careful not to minimize the seriousness of the matter by saying, "Everything is going to be fine." Rather, encourage them to pray.

Children need to understand that death is a part of life and nobody is going to live on this earth forever. Read Scriptures to them about death and the hereafter such as

Hebrews 9:27-28: "And just as each person is destined to die once and after that comes judgment, so also Christ died once for all time as a sacrifice to take away the sins of many people." Tell them about the beauty and joy in heaven where saved relatives go when they die. No need to exaggerate the awesomeness of it; just read Revelation 21:10-26 and 22:1-5 for the description.

Now, *how* you tell your small children to keep things in the family requires wisdom. They respond well to a visual comparison. "Johnny, some things we talk about *only* in our house because they are private. They are not for people who do not live here to hear about. It's like when you close the door when you go to the bathroom— because what goes on in there is private; it's not for everybody to know about."

You may also say such things as: "We aren't ready to share our news just yet, so please don't tell anyone until I say you can." "Every family has news or stories they only share with each other—this is one of them."

I caution you not to go overboard and teach your kids to be too secretive. You run the risk of producing children who are so private they rarely reveal any information about themselves—even to their close friends and later in life, their spouse. I've seen too many adults who have a huge problem with relational intimacy and transparency. Pray that God gives you the wisdom to teach your child how to have the balance between TMI and healthy discretion.

Day 15

Talking to God

"Therefore whoever humbles himself as this little child is the greatest in the kingdom of heaven."
MATTHEW 18:4 NKJV

Little Elise used to pray for the cups on the table, the bird sitting in the tree outside the kitchen window (her siblings accused her of not closing her eyes), each serving of food on her plate, the fact that her brother James could run really fast (and that she wanted to be fast too). Her wise single mom never made her feel that she was wasting God's valuable time praying for such things. There is no doubt that God was smiling because His precious Elise was comfortable being so conversational and personal.

That's what kids need to know about prayer—that it's just a conversation with God much like a conversation with Mommy or Daddy except that they can't see Him. Teaching your child to pray is the most significant form of communication he will ever engage in. Here's how you can succeed in this area.

Start early. Pray for your children before they are born. Pray over their crib. We live in troubled times and wise parents will plant the seeds of prayer in their kids from the beginning of their existence. They will do as the prophet Jeremiah admonished the Israelites to do after they had been captured by the Babylonians:

> Rise during the night and cry out.
>> Pour out your hearts like water to the Lord.
> Lift up your hands to him in prayer,
>> pleading for your children.
>
> (Lamentations 2:19)

Begin teaching kids to pray by leading them in prayer in the same simple communication style they use based on their stage of development:

"Thank you, God, for my food."

"God, please bless Mommy and Daddy."

"Lord, help me to make a good grade on my test."

Set the stage for them to believe in the power of God by explaining that, although He is invisible, He is present at all times and is much more powerful than any of their Superheroes, including Superman, Batman, Wonder Woman, Transformers, Power Rangers, and any others that captivate them.

Be consistent in praying with them. Pray with them each morning, at meal times, and before they go to bed. Pray a prayer of thanksgiving with them when good things happen and a prayer of petition when problems arise. Be quick to pray. When Little Salina comes to you and informs you of a problem, say, "Salina, why don't we pray right now for God to fix this." The more she sees this modeled, the more likely she will develop the habit of "real-time praying." This can also be a safeguard against your children treating God as a last resort instead of their first call. Depending on their age, ask your children to offer a short prayer for the situation before you offer your prayer.

Instruct them to pray for God's will to be done in their lives. Explain that God has a master plan for their lives and sometimes the thing they want may not be included in His plan. This is the time to trust the wisdom of the real Superhero.

Teach them how to exercise faith by speaking the promises of God as their personal truth. You can do this by reading simple Scriptures to them and helping them to "prayer-a-phrase" to make it personal. For example, Psalm 91 declares:

> If you make the LORD your refuge,
>   if you make the Most High your shelter,
> no evil will conquer you;
>   no plague will come near your home.
> For he will order his angels
>   to protect you wherever you go.
>
>   (Psalm 91:9-11)

You can coach your child to "prayer-a-phrase" the passage into a faith declaration: "Lord, I thank You that because I have made You my refuge and my shelter, You have ordered Your angels to protect me wherever I go." This type of praying can be a powerful tool that will bring your children peace throughout their lives.

Once you have your kids on the "prayer track,"

express your delight that they are praying. Let them know that you are confident God is honoring their prayers. Children are quick to believe since they have not learned the bad habits of worry, practical analysis of a troubling situation, and other hindrances to faith.

When teaching your children to pray, teach them to be:

Honest. Explain that God knows everything anyway, so it's useless to try to hide any negative behavior. Tell them to always ask forgiveness immediately for their wrongdoing. Let them know that God forgives us as soon as we repent; He doesn't need a cooling-off period before we can come back into His presence.

Expectant. Let them know that it is impossible to please God if they don't believe that He can answer their prayers (Hebrews 11:6). Only as kids become older does this become a problem. Wayne Holmes, compiler of *Whispering in God's Ear: True Stories Inspiring Childlike Faith*, believes the blind faith of children has a direct bearing on how God views their petitions: "Children seem to have a direct connection to heaven. Their earnest prayers demonstrate confidence in a heavenly Father whose tender reach extends to every corner of their world...Their unquestioning faith reveals the sort of simple trust many adults long to recapture in their own relationship with God." [11]

Humble. Teach your children that they get to come into God's presence because Jesus shed His blood to give us all direct access to Him. They should not think that because they have been a good boy or girl, they've earned brownie points and deserve His favor.

Thankful. Prayer isn't only about our requests; children need to learn to be grateful for what God has already done for them—even the little things. During times of prayer, instruct your child to name at least one specific thing she is grateful for.

Faithful and trusting. Inform your kids that God answers every prayer with yes, no, or wait. He won't always give them the answer they want…but He does answer, and we must trust Him to know what's best.

Parents, your children's knowledge that they can have a personal relationship with God through the blood of Jesus Christ and can come freely and frequently into His throne room is the most valuable gift you can give them.

Part Two

Triumphing Over
Negative Communication

Day 16

Lying

*"The LORD detests lying lips,
but he delights in those who tell the truth."*
PROVERBS 12:22

Six-year-old Jarret and four-year-old Sammy were playing together in a room across from where their mom was sewing when Sammy screamed out from obvious pain.

Sammy: "Mommy, Jarret hit me!"

Mom: "Jarret, did you hit your brother?"

Jarret: "No…"

Jarrett's response wasn't part of some deep, dark, well-thought-out plan of deception. The child simply made a quick assessment of the possible consequences of his actions and went into "punishment avoidance" mode.

Lying is probably one of the most difficult things to teach a child not to do. Hey, it's tough enough for adults! Think about how many times over the past few weeks you've told a little white lie, flattered somebody, exaggerated a reality, or told a half-truth. Lying seems to be a reflex action that's a part of our fallen nature.

The primary reason kids lie is to avoid negative consequences of their behavior: time-out, spanking, and loss of certain privileges. Your challenge as a parent is to train your children early on that there are better and more honorable ways to solve a problem than lying.

My hope is that you are raising your children to know and love the Lord. So the first step in dealing with your child's lying is to let him know that God really, really hates it (Proverbs 12:22) and that you want him to learn to hate what God hates.

Parents must impress upon children that lying will always have bad results. Even if they are never caught in the lie, they will not be happy on the inside if they have solved a problem with a lie (adults call this guilt and anxiety). The result of telling the truth may be unpleasant and even painful, but it is always honorable and right as it pleases God.

Of course, as a parent, you know the importance of setting a good example by telling the truth at all times. If you don't want to talk to someone on the phone, don't ask your children to tell the caller you are not home. Instead, simply instruct them to say you are unavailable. Don't promise your children you're going to take them somewhere or do something for them and never follow through. Instead, tell them you're going to try to make it happen or that if everything goes well, you will be able to do it. Don't tell every little girl who comes to the door selling cookies that you've already purchased some when you haven't. If you don't want to buy the cookies, simply say, "No, thank you."

Throw the door wide open for your children to step into the light of being truthful. Instead of directing angry accusations at them when you suspect them of not telling the truth, investigate the situation and seek to understand why they chose to resort to lying. In the absence of a smoking gun, listen and look for evidence. Is your child's version of the story credible? In telling his side, does his body language betray him? Can someone else corroborate his story? Be a cool investigator and ask questions such as, "Why did you hit your brother?" "Would you please explain why you didn't do your chores?" "What happened to cause you to break the lamp?"

These questions slam the door on an "I didn't do it" response. You have boldly indicated that you already *know* the truth of the situation. You are now simply getting clarification and giving them an opportunity to be heard, to present their case.

A great example of this approach is the story of Ananias and Sapphira (Acts 5:1-11). They lied about the amount of money they had received and passed on to the poor from the sale of their property. The apostle Peter, knowing they were lying, gave them space to explain their actions. They held fast to the lie, and God struck them dead on the spot!

When you question your kids in such a manner, hopefully you get responses such as:

- "I hit him because he tore my racetrack apart."
- "I didn't do my chores because I was talking to Kathleen on the phone."
- "I was running through the living room and ran into the lamp table."

Sometimes the only way for your kids to learn a lesson is the hard way.

Here's how nine-year-old Ethan's parents dealt with his lying. One day he stole a Matchbox car from a boy in his class at school. It was the coolest car he'd ever seen, and he wanted it more than anything. Ethan was normally a good kid, and it wasn't as if he didn't have plenty of the popular Matchbox cars and trucks of his own. When Ethan's mom picked him up from school, his teacher approached her about the missing car. She explained that one of the students said Ethan had taken it.

That evening Ethan's parents told him what the teacher had said, and eventually he confessed that he had taken the car. Then they told him he was going to give the car back to its rightful owner—immediately. Yes, they drove Ethan to the boy's house to apologize and give the car back. Further, he lost the privilege of playing with his own cars for a month.

Ethan was confronted in a non-angry way, required to make things right, and suffered a consequence for his actions. Oh, that every parent would practice the power of calm confrontation when their children lie. They will forge the truth-telling habit as they demonstrate the wisdom and courage to play the role of the "ICE" man or woman:

Instructor of strong moral principles

Coach for how to walk them out

Enforcer of age-appropriate consequences when they are violated

Day 17

Exaggerating

*"Deliver my soul, O LORD, from lying lips
And from a deceitful tongue."*
PSALM 120:2 NKJV

The dictionary defines *exaggerating* as "magnifying something beyond the limits of truth." Anything beyond the "limits of truth" is a lie. It's important to emphasize that because many people consider exaggerating a harmless activity. And exaggerating is not unique to children. I know several adults who constantly go beyond the "limits of truth" in relating their experiences or that of others.

Tell your kids about people who suffered negative consequences for exaggerating or lying. For younger children, you may want to stick with the story of the "Boy Who Cried Wolf." Just in case you've forgotten the details, the story is about a shepherd boy who would yell "Wolf! Wolf!" whenever he got bored. The people in the nearby village would come running—but there was never a wolf in sight. The boy would crack up laughing that they fell for his stunt time and again. One day a wolf actually came and attacked the sheep, but when the boy cried "Wolf! Wolf!" nobody came. When people know you constantly lie, they won't believe you even when you are telling the truth.

I have my share of adult exaggerators in my circle of interaction. I find it hard to have a serious conversation with them as I ponder how much of what they're saying I should believe versus how much to disregard. I am persuaded, however, that an exaggerating adult was once an exaggerating child. That's why it's important to nip this conduct in the bud before it gets entrenched. One distraught mother of an exaggerator cried out for help:

> My seven-year-old is exaggerating, and I am at my wits' end trying to figure out a way to stop this behavior. I want to get a handle on this so that he doesn't become a manipulator.
>
> He has had problems with some boys at school. I think in his effort to fit in he has discovered that some of the other students who tell tall tales are not held accountable, so he feels compelled to add his own exaggerated tales to fit in. For example, he has told the kids at school his dad drives a hot rod, which isn't true. He has also told teachers he has 13 cats. How can I stop this behavior? [1]

Sounds like this mom had a pretty good idea what was motiving her son's behavior—the desire for attention and the need for acceptance—the common thread among most exaggerators. What she was crying out for were some specific strategies for dealing with it. Here are my suggestions:

Don't set a bad example by being an exaggerator yourself. Be careful not to embellish your stories with superlative statements like "*Everybody* said…" or "*Nobody* wanted to…"

Don't ignore the exaggerations. If your kid is looking for attention, he is just going to tell bigger whoppers until he gets it.

Gently press the exaggerating child for specific details until her imagination runs dry. "So your friend Sally really has ten dogs? Are they all males? Can you describe them?" When she gets frustrated because she can't answer any more, call her on it. "I believe you are stretching the facts. I need you to understand that God doesn't like that and neither do I." Now would be a good time to tell her a "negative consequence" story and emphasize that exaggerating is lying.

If you have facts that refute his exaggeration, *correct him immediately*—even in the presence of others. "Actually, Timmy, I believe what really happened is…" This teaches him that if you discover he is exceeding the limits of the truth, you will not help him save face by going along with him.

Give him a taste of his own medicine. Blogger Wannikki Taylor posted a great suggestion on how to do so:

> Give your child an exaggerated story of a treat you will give him as an afternoon snack for the day. Tell him that the snack will be a candied apple dipped in caramel with tons of sprinkles and a glass of strawberry milkshake. Instead of giving him a candied apple and a milkshake, place a simple apple and cup of milk in front of him. He'll ask why you're giving him a snack

that's far short of what you promised. Explain to him that though exaggeration makes something sound good, it distorts the truth and can leave a person disappointed.[2]

Applaud him when he relates a story accurately. Let him know that you are proud of his truth-telling. Lying has its penalties and truth has its rewards.

Make sure that you *set aside some specific, quality time for your child* so that he knows he is loved, valued, and accepted just the way he is.

Day 18

Sassing Parents

*"A child who is allowed to be disrespectful to his
parents will not have true respect for anyone."*
BILLY GRAHAM, EVANGELIST

"You know," eleven-year-old Raye confided, "my parents say that I'm disrespectful. I don't know what they mean. It's not like somebody sat down and explained what's disrespectful!" Raye is a good kid, but she does indeed talk back to her mom and dad with little restraint and no consequences. I've witnessed it up close and personal.

I think she makes a good point though. Parents must be diligent in teaching their kids what constitutes disrespect. I'm not suggesting that you develop a long list of dos and don'ts. However, the moment disrespect rears its ugly head, whether in tone or in words, it needs to be addressed.

Many modern parents believe if they just ignore it, it will eventually go away. Not so. The old adage "Silence is consent" has never been more true. If you don't nip disrespect in the bud, it will grow like a weed. Just the other day, a close friend was bemoaning how disrespectfully her twenty-six-year-old daughter had spoken to her.

Then she confessed, "Of course, she's always been a little sassy. But this time was really bad."

A kid who talks back is a product of tolerant parents (or single parent) who wouldn't set boundaries with appropriate and consistent consequences. We teach kids (and others) how to treat us by what we tolerate. Yes, I know we live in stressful times and that most parents experience pressure and drama on their jobs. Many are loath to add more tension to their home life by disciplining a child who will probably not respond well to it—especially when she's used to leniency.

A significant number of disrespectful kids talk back because the parent has lost credibility with them. Being credible means you are trustworthy, believable, and reliable. As a parent, you *must* maintain credibility with your children if you have any hope at all of raising them to be obedient, trustworthy, and reliable adults. It is something your children have to see you model consistently. If you don't say what you mean nor mean what you say, and if you model a life of compromised morals (in their opinion), it won't take long before your children feel justified in disrespecting you.

To bring up your children in a home where respect is expected and experienced, try these proven strategies:

• Think before you pronounce punishment. Threatening your children with no television for a month or being grounded for six months or going to bed before dark for the rest of the year is unrealistic.

- Don't assume you are always right.

- Don't hesitate to admit to your children when you are wrong and apologize for any shortcoming on your part, such as overreacting.

- Once you make a judgment call or a promise to discipline your child, don't back down; stay the course (unless you get new information that negates what you based your decision on). This is why it is best to think before you speak.

- Don't allow your children to watch television shows and movies that portray parents as clueless, immature, and wishy-washy.

- Have zero tolerance for lying and deception.

- Establish expectations and guidelines that are consistent and ongoing rather than off the cuff and based upon your mood.

The results of being a credible parent include:

Providing your children with the safety net they need and want. It lets them know where their boundaries are and what will happen when they step over those boundaries (and we all know that kids will test the limits).

Saving time and energy better spent on talking and listening rather than arguing and fighting emotional battles. Instead of engaging in skirmishes of words and wills, you can reason with them, listen to them, and plant in their minds that you are the parent. While there are times you are open to negotiation and compromise, once you set the boundaries, they are going to remain set.

While it is best to begin your parenting adventure as a credible parent, you may be reading this at your kid's post-toddler stage. If so, don't worry—just start now. If your children are over the age of four or five, sit them down and explain in a calm, nondefensive, and age-appropriate manner how and why things are going to be different going forward. Be very specific on the guidelines: no raising their voices to you, no walking away when you are speaking to them. Tell them that this doesn't mean they cannot ask questions, ask for compromise, or suggest alternatives—but you always have the final say. The end.

Finally, emphasize to your kids that you love them dearly and desire to see them have the long and prosperous life God has promised to children who honor their parents. This may be a good time to print out this promise and have them read and memorize it. Framing it would be a cool thing to do also.

> Children, obey your parents because you belong to the Lord, for this is the right thing to do. "Honor your father and mother." This is the first commandment with a promise: If you honor your father and mother, "things will go well for you, and you will have a long life on the earth" (Ephesians 6:1-3).

Day 19

Manipulating

*Manipulate: to influence or control
someone cleverly, skillfully, or deviously.*

Once I was playing with my neighbor's four-year-old daughter, Stacy, who was fascinated by my colorful necklace. She toyed with it a while as I held her on my lap. Then she moved in for the kill. She put her arms around my neck and said to me very sweetly, "You are so pretty. Can I have your necklace?"—all in the same breath!

Stacy was too innocent to hide her ulterior motive with more finesse, but smart enough to know that saying nice things to people would likely get her what she wanted. Of course, not one to be manipulated by the little cherub-faced beauty, I kept my necklace.

Children have a variety of strategies they use to manipulate parents or people outside the home into giving them what they want. Let's see if you can identify which ones your child favors and what you can do to stop this habit in its tracks.

Flattery. When your kid gives you an over-the-top compliment ("You're the best mom in the whole world!"), just say "Thank you. I appreciate hearing that." When he follows it up a few minutes or hours later with a problematic request, know that you have been set up to be manipulated. Don't let the fear of not living up to his accolade force you to say yes when a wiser answer is "No—but I'm glad I'm the best mom in the world!"

Irrational arguments. "Why can't I stay up and watch a movie on a school night. I made an *A* on my math quiz, plus I make my bed every morning!" Don't argue the irrelevance of his facts to his request. Respond like a parent, not a peer. "Because I think it's best that you get enough sleep. Good night."

Fake crying. Toddlers have perfected this one. I have babysat kids who would yell at the top of their voices with no tears in their eyes. They just seem to know instinctively that you will want to stop the annoying sound. Well, strong parent, look that little darling straight in the eyes and say, "I can't hear your words when you're crying. If you want something, ask me this way…" Then give him a script so that he learns how to ask for what he wants in a more powerful and effective way: "Mom, I'd like…"

Pitting Mom and Dad against each other. "But Mom said I could spend the night with Suzie." Okay, Mom and Dad, unite! Decide ahead of time what decisions will require your mutual consent: all social activities (including slumber parties), adjustments to weekly allowances, certain purchases (cell phones, computers, electronics). This is critical to your own quality of life. Failure to walk in agreement here will destroy your marriage. The behavior will only get worse during the teen years.

When your kid comes to you and tries to appeal a decision your spouse has made, don't take the bait. Turn the tables. "What did your mom/dad say?" Even if you do not agree with your spouse's decision, you may have to accept it for a show of solidarity. Now, for goodness sake, don't compete with each other for your kid's favor by being the yes-man or yes-woman. This happens frequently with parents who are separated or divorced. No matter how messy the separation was, focus on the higher goal of raising a great kid who knows he can't always have his way.

Threatening to run away. School-age kids (and teens for sure) can be adept at using this tactic to get their way. Sometimes they actually follow through, so be wise here. National Runaway Safeline (www.1800runaway.org) consultant Joel Kessel advises that if your child threatens to run away, you should sit him down and talk to him about what is prompting the threat: "Invite him to talk with you or someone else about what is troubling him and be supportive of finding positive ways of dealing with his situation."

Natalia Bruen, whose ten-year-old son actually ran away from home, says, "I really think it's important to be calm and not be too indulgent sometimes. I explain to my son that his place is home until he's an adult, and that the world is wonderful, but also a scary place when you are a child. You need the protection of your family, even if you don't always like us."

Playing the victim. "I never get to do anything I want." Your response: "I'm sorry you feel that way." Rattle off a list of benefits and privileges she enjoys but obviously does not appreciate.

Playing sick. Because kids are great observers of what works and what doesn't, there is a good chance your child may feign sickness to get more attention or to avoid an unpleasant task. Be a discerning parent and watch the signals. Try to schedule some one-on-one time with her but not in the current moment lest she think her tactics worked. *Caution*: Don't be too quick to dismiss the "sickness." Check your child's temperature and look for other signs of common childhood illnesses.

Pouting/looking sad. Yes, you'd like to see your kid look happy 24/7, but in every life some rain must fall. See the discussion in chapter 25, "Pouting."

Temper tantrums and angry outbursts. Most kids are banking on your desire to avoid such unpleasantness. Surprise them and implement undesirable consequences for manipulative behavior. See the discussion in chapter 21, "Tantrums and Angry Outbursts."

Parents, do not let your fear of alienation or disconnection from your child cause you to cave in to her manipulative behavior. You are training a future adult. You cannot afford to send your child out into the world believing that manipulation is an effective way to get what she wants. So what that it worked for Delilah in getting Samson to reveal the secret to his strength (Judges 16:4-21). She was hardly the model of integrity. Instead, be diligent in pointing out to your kid when she is being manipulative. Remind her that people do not embrace those who use such evil persuasion; no one likes feeling they have been played. Encourage her to communicate her desires clearly and directly.

Finally, teach your child to focus on genuinely serving people and showing such care and concern that when the time comes that he needs a favor, people will gladly reciprocate. I know this firsthand. During the writing of this book, the brother of our friend Ralph passed away. Ralph and his wife, Cathy, have so much "goodwill on the books" with Darnell and me and a community of others, we all felt supporting them in practical and tangible ways during their time of grief was the least we could do—despite our busy schedules and critical deadlines.

Day 20

Disrespecting Authority

*"Respect for ourselves guides our morals;
respect for others guides our manners."*
LAURENCE STERNE, ANGLICAN CLERGYMAN

My friend C.L., a prekindergarten teacher, told me about two four-year-old girls she'd given a cup of water to during recess. They were dawdling and having fun holding the water in their filled-to-capacity jaws. After waiting patiently, C.L. asked them to go ahead and swallow the water. One little girl obeyed. However, Little Sally spat her water directly onto C.L.'s pants and shoes. C.L. immediately took her to the principal's office.

When Sally's mother arrived to pick her up, the staff informed her of the incident. She was livid that the teacher had sent Sally to the principal's office rather than putting her in a time-out. She refused to require Sally to apologize because, first of all, she "didn't see her do it" and second, "a four-year-old is too young to understand what it means to apologize." Sally's mom missed a critical opportunity to teach behavioral boundaries and respect for adults. She chose rather to blame the victim for her daughter's unacceptable behavior.

One of the most important things you can teach your child is where respect ends and disrespect begins. *Respect* is "deference to another person's authority or admiration for another person." Teaching your children to respect authority happens by doing three things:

1. living respectfully yourself and letting them see that you do

2. implementing a negative consequence for being disrespectful

3. treating your children with respect

Let's look at these three essentials in more detail.

Live Respectfully

You've heard the adage, "Do as I say, not as I do." Many compromising parents resort to this expression to justify their own questionable behavior. Parents that embrace this saying produce kids who are confused, frustrated, anxious, and all-too-often rebellious against authority. That's why living respectfully is essential in teaching your children to respect authority. You may be saying to yourself right about now, *Hey, I'm a law-abiding citizen. I don't cheat on my income taxes, and I've never stolen anything in my life.* Go, you! But ask yourself, do you:

• drive over the speed limit

• speak to your spouse disrespectfully

- talk negatively about your child's mother or father
- treat wait staff or store clerks rudely
- talk on your cell phone in a public place that may cause disruption
- speak rudely to telemarketers rather than simply saying, "No, thank you," and hanging up
- bad-mouth your boss or demean her ability
- leave a mess in store dressing rooms or disarrange items on shelves or displays

While these things may seem irrelevant or trivial to teaching your child respect, they aren't. They are full-fledged examples of disrespect and rebellion that you unwittingly pass on to your children.

Josh's parents just didn't understand why their clean-cut, golf star, honor-student son was taken into custody after being stopped for speeding. They argued with the police officer (in front of Josh) that he was only going eight miles over the speed limit. The officer explained that "only eight miles" was still speeding and that it was in a school zone. But, he went on to say, the reason he took Josh down to the station and called his parents was because Josh had demonstrated such a disrespectful attitude, telling the officer he could do a better job by going after the potheads instead of bothering him.

Josh's parents had raised him to believe he was better than others. Because he excelled in certain areas, they overlooked the things he did wrong. Josh and his parents felt that it was not necessary to respect the officer's authority because other kids were doing worse things than what Josh was doing. Tell that to the parents of the child Josh could easily have injured speeding through a school zone.

Implement Consequences

If there are no consequences for their actions, your children will never learn to respect authority—yours or anyone else's. Once again, I am reminded of a Berenstain Bears story. Mama Bear was a wise parent. When Sister Bear asked to go to Lizzy's sleepover, Mama told her that allowing her to go was a privilege and that with privilege comes the responsibility of being on her best behavior and being responsible.

Because Lizzy's parents were not home to supervise, things got out of hand. The noise got too loud and the neighbor called the police—who happened to arrive just as Lizzy's parents returned home. They cancelled the party and called the parents to pick up their children.

Mama Bear was very angry. She lectured Sister Bear on how disappointed she was at Sister's lack of respect and responsibility. She also grounded Sister from her favorite activities. She even took her back to Lizzy's house the next morning to be part of the clean-up brigade. She figured if Sister Bear helped to make the mess, she needed to help clean it up.[3] Consequences for actions.

One of the worst things you can ever do to your children is to rescue them from the consequences of their behavior. Consequences are a natural cause and effect. Therefore, if you allow your children to cause something but never allow them to experience the effect, they will never know or understand what it means to be accountable or responsible.

Respect Your Children

Children are people too. They feel, think (sometimes), have dreams, get scared—everything you and I do, including wanting respect. They need you as a parent to respect them by:

- being considerate and conscious of their feelings
- allowing them an appropriate amount of privacy
- giving their thoughts and opinions consideration whenever possible
- apologizing to them when you are wrong
- allowing them space to grow into who they are—not who you think they should be (as long as it is safe, legal, and healthy)

How your children respect authority speaks volumes about their home training. Respecting authority doesn't mean your child must always agree with the powers that be, but he is willing to defer to their authority for the good of all involved. Further, it shows an ability to compromise and to take the proper and respectful channels to bring about change.

Day 21

Tantrums and Angry Outbursts

"A gentle answer deflects anger,
but harsh words make tempers flare."
PROVERBS 15:1

As a little girl—and even into her teens—when Crystal felt she was being treated unfairly, she would clinch her fists and say, "Not fair! Not fair! Not fair!" She'd get louder each time, the last time yelling at the top of her lungs. She wanted whoever was on the receiving end to know that she was not happy and thought yelling got the point across. Children yell in anger for a number of reasons:

- They're simply imitating their parents. If you are a yeller, your children will probably be yellers too.

- They've learned that they aren't heard unless they yell.

- They feel helpless. Children who yell in anger may be expressing a far deeper anger or frustration than just with the situation that sparked the outburst.

Frustration is usually the reason for toddler temper tantrums. Of course, there are the spoiled brats who throw fits because they know they work. Notwithstanding, smart parents will be careful not to set themselves up for a tantrum by poor planning. If you haven't fed the little darling in several hours, chances are she is going to get hungry on your trip to the market. That could spell trouble as she is surrounded by things to eat. Yelling may be the quickest way to say, "I need food!"

Now, I'm from the "you teach by what you tolerate" school of thought. Therefore, know that you are setting a precedent when you cave in to a child's tantrums or angry outbursts. Instead, try these strategies to come out of a tantrum with your sanity intact.

Do not administer corporal punishment in public. This is not the place or the time to spank your child (these days, someone may report you for abuse!). I hate it when a parent takes extreme discipline measures to impress onlookers when it is clear to all that such discipline doesn't happen at home. It's just best to leave where you are, even if you have to take the kid kicking and screaming.

If your child is old enough to talk, encourage her to tell you what's bothering her. "Use your voice to tell Mommy what's wrong. I can't hear your voice if you are screaming." God forbid that you raise a child who thinks she can bully her parent by yelling.

Set clear boundaries and don't budge from them. "Jessie, if you don't stop screaming, I'm going to put back the Fruit Loops we just bought for you."

Have your child agree to a plan. When I would take my niece to the park to feed the ducks, she always cried and screamed when I tried to get her to leave. So I started telling her as soon as we arrived, "When we have given the ducks all the popcorn, we are going to leave the park. If you cry, we will have to stop coming to the park for a long, long time." It took a while to get her to cooperate fully, but I won the contest of wills.

Use your voice. Be calm and authoritative. Follow up threats with age-appropriate consequences. No need for you to scream too. Remember that you are the parent, not a peer.

The main lesson here is to teach your children that yelling is not an appropriate or effective way to express their anger or to get their needs met. If a child doesn't feel the need to yell in order to be heard, he won't yell. When you provide a home in which children and adults alike are able to share their feelings—good, bad, or indifferent—in a calm, reasonable manner, they will do so. If your child knows he can come to you, tell you he is angry (even if he is angry with *you*), and that you will really listen, he won't feel the need to shout his feelings above the silence of being ignored or the noise of everyone else being heard.

There are times, however, when letting off some steam is just the thing a child needs. Consider Evan's story. He lost his dad when he was twelve, and he was angry with his dad for leaving him. He was also angry with himself for not being there when he died. Evan was angry at the world. For a long time, he stuffed his anger deep inside. He thought he had to be "the man" for his mom and two younger brothers. Four year later when his mom remarried, he got angry with her for "forgetting" his dad. Even though he liked the man she married and was glad to see her happy, he was still angry. But he never said a word.

One night at church camp, he and some of his lifelong friends were talking to their youth sponsor about their fears when Evan's feelings came pouring out. He was afraid of his anger. He was afraid to let it loose and afraid of facing it. The youth sponsor encouraged him to yell and scream and let it all out in a place where he felt completely safe. She suggested digging a hole, screaming and yelling into it, and then covering it back over— burying the anger once and for all. When Evan returned home he did just that. He said he'd never felt such release in all his years.

There are times when blowing off some steam may be therapeutic for your child. As long as he does not direct it toward anyone and does not hurt someone or himself, let him go for it.

Teaching a child to express his frustration openly, honestly, and calmly will also equip him to resolve his feelings rationally rather than acting without thinking. When it comes to resolving anger, admonish your child to taking a deep breath, count to ten, and use his indoor voice. This is a winning strategy.

Day 22

Cursing

*"Don't use foul or abusive language. Let
everything you say be good and helpful."*
EPHESIANS 4:29

Grandpa John took four-year-old Mackenzie to the
hospital cafeteria to eat and to distract her from baby sister's anxiety-filled hospital room. Because Mackenzie's
parents farmed with her grandparents, Grandpa knew
exactly what to say to get her mind off what was happening on the fourth floor.

"How are your baby lambs?" he asked.

"Good," she replied. "But we have to do something
to get rid of those #$@&%* coyotes!"

There were some older ladies in the room whose
heads snapped around when they heard the profanity.

Grandpa John raised his eyebrows. "What did you
say?"

Mackenzie innocently repeated her statement word
for word. She was simply repeating what she'd heard her
father say in a moment of frustration.

Most parents have had their "hospital cafeteria"
moments. Even if you don't use foul language yourself,

chances are your children will pick up a word or two on the school bus, at the childcare center, or from Uncle Ralph. So what's a parent to do?

Mind your mouth! Whether it's good manners, respect, or any other conduct, the adage "monkey see, monkey do" certainly applies here. Children *do* what they *see* and *say* what they *hear*. The most effective way to teach your children to refrain from profanity is to lead the way.

Establish what constitutes a bad word. In some families, *butt* is the acceptable replacement for the other word; in other families, it is considered discipline-worthy. As your children become more socially active, spending time with friends and at school, they are going to be exposed to different opinions of what a bad word is and what's allowed between siblings and what's not. That's why it is important to establish your family's guidelines and expectations early on.

Respond to profanity immediately. Worldly wisdom says to not act shocked or overreact. I say, yes, remain calm but for goodness' sake, don't act like nothing has happened. I'm a firm believer that we *teach* children how to behave by what we *tolerate*. A child must immediately be told that profanity is unacceptable and will not be tolerated. How to do that varies depending on the child's state of development. Behavior professor Dr. Timothy Jay asserts,

> Egocentric young children do not fully comprehend why words are offensive to listeners, but can be trained not to use offensive words. One

might simply tell a two- to three-year-old not to use a word without much explanation. Five-year-olds, on the other hand, can be given an explanation for language restrictions. The eight-year-old is capable of empathy and is able to see that words can hurt others' feelings.[4]

Explain why cursing is bad. Telling preschoolers like Mackenzie that they shouldn't say certain words will usually work as long as they are not being repeatedly exposed to such language. But inevitably your children will encounter profanity…perhaps regularly. As a parent, you need to take the time to explain why bad words are inappropriate. Make sure you explain:

- Cursing is unacceptable to God (Ephesians 4:29).

- Cursing is offensive and disrespectful.

- Cursing is disdained by people important to them, such as teachers and, later, employers.

Offer alternatives to bad words. Many years ago, my now-deceased mother regularly babysat her granddaughter Ashley. Mom was a devout Christian and delighted in teaching her grandkids the Bible and how to be a godly person. She taught Ashley about that horrible Jezebel and all the mean kings. As far as Ashley was concerned, these were the most despicable people ever. One day, somebody really upset her. At the height of her frustration, she shouted, "You Jezebel! You mean king!" That was her alternative to profanity. She is now over thirty-years-old with a school-age son she is teaching not to repeat bad words.

When we get angry or scared we often search for words to express our feelings "to the max." Some parents offer their children alternative words to use when they really want to express their frustration while keeping their language in check. Some families pick silly words or even make up their own words to use in place of cuss words. Here are a few that some people say they use: "Fig tree!" (based on the story in Matthew 21:18-22 of Jesus cursing the fig tree because it yielded no fruit), "Oh, chicken feet!," and "Shahka mahka!" (Hey, don't knock 'em; these expressions are a lot better than cursing.)

The important thing is to teach your kids that whatever is in our hearts determines what we say (Matthew 12:33-37). Therefore, their goal must be to prevent attitudes and words that are dishonoring from taking root in their hearts.

Establish and follow through on consequences for using profanity. Washing their mouths out with soap is an oldie but goodie. Being "servant for a day" to the sibling who was on the receiving end of a bad word or name-calling is another effective consequence. Other penalties some parents say they have used include:

- saying the bad word one hundred times so they get sick of saying it (ummm, not too sure about that one)

- writing an age-appropriate number of nice words

- not allowing the offender to speak for the rest of the day or evening

- requiring them to write out and memorize Psalm 39:1 (NKJV): "I will guard my ways, lest I sin with my tongue," or Psalm 19:14: "May the words of my mouth and the meditation of my heart be pleasing to you, O LORD, my rock and my redeemer."

Help your child develop and use a vocabulary of "feeling" words. Rather than cursing, they can learn to express their frustration by saying such things as: "I'm angry," "I'm disgusted," "I'm annoyed." Many parents resort to profanity because they simply have no other words to convey the intensity of their thoughts or emotions. Thus, the cursing habit is passed on to their kids.

I say it's time to teach kids that cursing is a sign of a limited supply of power words and not evidence of being powerful.

Tattling

"He who goes about as a talebearer reveals secrets,
But he who is trustworthy conceals a matter."
Proverbs 11:13 nasb

"When Joseph was seventeen years old, he often tended his father's flocks. He worked for his half brothers...But Joseph reported to his father some of the bad things his brothers were doing" (Genesis 37:2). Joseph's brothers resented tattling and later sold him into slavery. He was a captive for thirteen years before a series of providential events landed him in the position of prime minister of Egypt (Genesis 41). There are several tattle-tales in the Bible, and oddly, they were not children (see Daniel 6 and Esther 3).

But it's natural for small children to tattle. They do it for a couple of reasons. First, they're just learning to recognize conflict and don't know how to resolve it, so they come to you—their hero and safety net. Second, they are eager to please you and feel that letting you know that *they* know right from wrong will get them some brownie points. It's how they strut their moral compass.

Neither of these reasons is malicious or mean-spirited.

That's why it is important that you *not* respond as if they are. If you say, "Don't be a tattletale," "No one is going to want to play with you if you're always telling on them," or "Just ignore them and go on," you are sending the message that you are not concerned about their sense of fairness. On the other hand, you also don't want to rush right in and fix the problem for them. You won't always be around to do that. Remember, they are learning to *socialize*—a fancy word for getting along with people. What is important, however, is that you listen to every word they say, then help them learn how to come to a "tattle" or "tell" decision.

One Canadian municipality has put forth a very simple explanation of the difference between tattling and telling:

- *Tattling* is trying to get someone *into* trouble when no one is being hurt and no rule is being broken.

- *Telling* is trying to get someone *out of* trouble by getting help when there are unsafe behaviors.[5]

To make sure you're clear on the difference, let's take a little test. Read the following examples and decide whether each is a case of "tattling" or "telling."

1. Your house rule is no sweets between meals. Your son catches your daughter eating a candy bar and runs to you with the information.

2. You give your three children a large bottle of bubble mixture, three wands, and three small

bowels to pour their individual mixtures. One of the children comes running inside with the news that the oldest of the three poured the bubbles, giving herself the most "because I'm the oldest."

3. Your daughter and her friends are in the mall, and one of the girls decides to shoplift. Your daughter tells the girl that if she does, she will tell the store clerk.

4. Your son tells his friend Sam that he'd told you about Sam's talk of committing suicide. Sam gets angry and refuses to talk to him.

5. Your twelve-year-old tells you and your spouse that he saw your older daughter and her boyfriend kissing.

Well, let's see how you did. The correct answers in order are: tattling, tattling, telling, telling, tattling.

It's fairly easy to see the difference in each of these situations, especially as adults. But it's not always so easy for your children to distinguish between *tattling* and *telling*. Wise parents teach their kids when it's important to *tell*—to report certain situations to them or to another adult in a position of authority. Here are some examples:

- A kid brings a knife, gun, or other weapon to school.

- A friend confides that she is thinking of hurting a classmate.

- You or a friend or classmate is being bullied.

- You witness a friend purging her food each day after lunch.

- A friend or classmate has agreed to meet a stranger who befriended her on the Internet.

Another important alternative to tattling is to teach your children to tell someone directly if their behavior is having a negative effect on them. For example: "Could you please stop kicking my chair?" No need to get an adult involved unless he won't stop.

A final alternative is just to walk away. Teach your child that if they don't "have a dog in the fight" (nothing to lose personally), and there is no potential danger or harm to anybody, teach them to say to themselves, *This is not my business. I'm out!*

By teaching children at an early age to make the distinction between tattling and telling, you will be keeping the lines of communication open. By giving them alternatives to tattling (problem-solving skills and the confidence to sometimes walk away), you are building their character and confidence, making them less vulnerable to peer pressure. By letting them know you are there to listen, advise, and lend a hand when necessary, you are building a strong relationship that will be priceless in the years to come.

Day 24

Spreading Rumors and Gossip

*"A gossip goes around telling secrets,
so don't hang around with chatterers."*
PROVERBS 20:19

We used to play a game in grade school called "Telephone." Our class of about twenty-five students would sit in a circle. The teacher would start at the beginning of the circle and whisper a statement to the first student, who would then whisper it to the next until it reached the last student, who would then repeat aloud what the statement was. It was *never* the same as the beginning statement.

The teacher may have started out by saying "The general is sending reinforcements; we are going to advance." However, by the time it reached the last person, the message may have changed to "Jimmy went to the Air Force and now he's going to a dance." We always got a good laugh at how twisted the final version was.

Rumors are like that; however, they are no laughing matter. When information passes from one person to another, it is bound to get distorted. Good parents will teach their kids not to *initiate* or *participate* in a rumor chain or a gossip fest. Just for clarity, let me make explain the difference between a rumor and gossip. A rumor is *unverified* information passed from person to person; gossip is idle talk about the often *verified,* but always private, affairs of another.

Parents really set the pace for how their kids handle information about other people. I read a story recently about a woman whose ten-year-old son overheard her and her friend gossiping about an inappropriate outfit his friend Jack's mom had worn to a school function. Later he asked her why she was saying "such mean things" about Jack's mom when he thought they were friends. Fortunately, this mom had the humility to admit that her behavior was wrong and that she was going to be more mindful in the future not to talk behind someone's back. She was merely having a light "bonding moment" with her friend, but she ended up setting a bad example for her son.

Kids traffic in rumors and gossip for various reasons: for attention as the "one with the scoop," to be a part of the in-crowd, to reduce the status or mar the image of someone they envy, or to retaliate against someone who has offended them, to name a few. Whatever their motivation, the most important thing to teach your kids is that spreading rumors and gossip is not pleasing to God and it hurts.

Gossip starts creeping into girls' conversations about

the time they turn twelve; boys may gossip also, but they usually don't gain status this way.

Here are some key gossip-busting strategies you can employ as a parent.

Don't participate in gossip yourself—as a receiver or carrier of juicy information. Therefore, when someone (even your best friend) starts gossiping about a person, simply change the subject or muster the courage to say, "We'd better not talk about that." Most gossipers won't appreciate the rebuke, but you must be steadfast in your resolve to let the words of your mouth be acceptable in God's sight.

Let your kids see gossip's impact. Most kids do not fully understand how harmful and mean gossip is. Find articles for them to read about children who hurt and even killed themselves after being the target of malicious gossip. Watch movies such as *Mean Girls, Never Been Kissed,* and *Thirteen Going on Thirty* with your daughters to show them how dangerous gossip can be.

Teach them to do a quick "self-audit" when tempted to pass on negative information about another kid by asking themselves these questions:

- What is my real reason or motive for wanting to share this information with others?

- Is this going to hurt or tarnish the person's reputation, image, or status?

- If I were the subject of the rumor or gossip, how would I feel about others talking about this?

- How will I respond if the person confronts me about my role in passing this information on?

- Even if I do not pass this on to others, what else can I do (such as speaking up for the person) to halt any negative impact this may have?

If you catch your child in the act of gossiping, *require her to apologize to the person she has maligned* and to let others know she was wrong. Monitor your kid's computer (yes, get the password) for evidence of cyber-gossiping.

Use an object lesson to help your child understand the results of gossip. Here's an activity that Tamara Chilver, homeschooler and founder of Teaching with TLC, suggests for helping your child understand the results of gossip.

> Give your child a tube of toothpaste and a paper plate. Have him squeeze some of the toothpaste onto the plate. Now, tell your child to put the toothpaste back into the tube. After they try to accomplish this nearly impossible task, explain that once our words leave our mouths, we can never take them back.
>
> Read Luke 6:45: "The good man brings good things out of the good stored up in his heart, and the evil man brings evil things out of the evil stored up in his heart. For out of the overflow of his heart his mouth speaks."
>
> Make the point that just as the toothpaste came from inside the tube through the "mouth" of the tube, the thoughts that come from our hearts go through

our mouths. What we say is a reflection of what is in our hearts.[6]

Remind them often that *initiating* or *participating* in gossip or rumors will cause many to mistrust them as a potential friend and others to simply avoid them. Emphasize to your kids that talking about someone else's life won't make their life any better. In fact, it can make it worse since it takes away the energy they could be using to pursue their divine purpose.

Impress upon your kids the principle that you reap what you sow. One who gossips will always end up being gossiped about. Admonish them that those who gossip *with* you will surely gossip *about* you.

In your daily prayer with your kids, pray that they will honor God in all they do and *say*.

Pouting

Pout: to show disappointment, anger,
or resentment, usually in silence.

Gabrielle's mother, Victoria, was proud that her children did not misbehave in public. It was no accident, though. Victoria always told Gabrielle and her older sister what she expected of them—when shopping, she would not tolerate yelling, begging, crying, pouting, and running around in stores under any circumstances. Victoria knew that children thrive on knowing what their boundaries are and what the consequences will be when they violate them. But you know what they say, even the best laid plans can go awry.

One day Gabrielle came home from school declaring she just had to have a certain pair of boots. She talked nonstop about them, practically begging her mom to take her to the mall to get them. Victoria finally agreed to go the next evening. "But," she said, "I'm not making any promises to buy them." When Victoria saw the price of the boots was eighty dollars, she told Gabrielle they were too expensive for their budget. Further, Victoria thought the boots were not practical for school—even if every other mom thought so.

This was not the first time Victoria had told Gabrielle no. But this was the first time Gabrielle reacted by crying, pouting, and refusing to talk as they left the mall and drove home. When she finally did speak, her attitude was rude and disrespectful.

Victoria let her have her space. The next day, she told Gabrielle that she could save her own money and buy the boots if they were that important to her. A few years previous, Gabrielle had saved to buy her American Girl doll. She'd paid half and her parents had matched it. *That 50-50 thing might work this time too*, Gabrielle thought.

But when she proposed the idea, Victoria promptly said no. Victoria calmly said to her, "That is not an option because you pouted and misbehaved when you couldn't have your way. If you'd acted differently, a 50-50 arrangement would have been okay."

Pouting had cost Gabrielle something she really wanted. Good job, Victoria.

Pouting starts early in life. As a nonparent, I used to find it odd that small children think they are punishing their parents or teaching them a lesson by giving them the silent treatment. *How can a little bit of peace and quiet be punishment?* Through observation, research, and childsitting, I've now learned that it is indeed a form of punishment as most parents do not want to experience the discomfort and alienation of a pouting kid.

Kids know this instinctively. They want what they want and they will manipulate to get it. However, if you cater to their pouting, they are going to miss one of the most critical lessons for later in life—they won't always get what they want. Further, not everyone is going to cater to their emotional blackmail. Some insecure folks may for fear of losing connection, but most will not.

So, just let them pout. Leaving kids to think things through isn't a bad thing. If you try to make them speak before they are ready, you're just asking for another battle.

Caution: You cannot allow your child to defy you by remaining silent when you ask him a direct question. If your toddler refuses to answer you, simply put him in time-out and take away all toys and privileges until he responds.

Once your children have passed toddlerhood and early preschool years, you will find it necessary to address again the silent-treatment issue. Here are some recommendations for how best to handle the silent treatment from older children.

Understand that when kids (and adults) pout, they are banking on your inability to handle the guilt and discomfort of seeing them suffer sadness. Let them have their moment.

They need to understand that you are *allowing* them this time rather than believing they are punishing you or have the upper hand. "I'll give you some time to think about what's going on, but we are going to talk about this later." You also need to let them know that keeping silent isn't going to make the problem better or make it go away. They must learn to use words to express their desires.

Don't respond to their silence by being silent. Retaliating with your own silence is childish and immature. Act like a parent, not a peer.

Give your children a reason to want to talk to you. By consistently working to keep the lines of communication open and by proving you are a trustworthy listener, you will open the door for your children to come to you. You can also share a few words of wisdom about how opening up and talking will enable both of you to find the best solution to the problem.

Be approachable. This goes hand in hand with giving your children a reason to want to talk, but it's a bit deeper than that. Giving your children the assurance that you are not going to overreact, explode, accuse, or fly off the handle makes them feel safe…comfortable…willing.

It is up to you as a parent to teach the value of both silence and conversation and how to keep them in their proper place. You don't want your child to grow up to be a selfish, manipulating person whose only concern is his own welfare and desires. This makes for miserable relationships in marriage, the workplace, and in other social interactions.

Whining

*"Do everything without
complaining and arguing."*
PHILIPPIANS 2:14

Kids whine because the little rascals know it usually works! Now, if you are the type of parent who is easily worn down and usually gives in to this aggravating, annoying, and obnoxious habit, then you are perpetuating the problem. Whining is typically more than just annoying though; it's often an indication that something is wrong. You'll be wise to make note of the circumstances to see if the whining is an outward expression of one or more of the following conditions.

Exhaustion. Has your child gotten enough rest or has he had a couple of later-than-usual nights? If so, make sure he gets plenty of sleep.

Illness. When a child doesn't feel well, he isn't always capable of communicating this. He could be coming down with a cold, the flu, an earache, chicken pox, or some other childhood ailment. Find out how he's feeling.

Hunger. Perhaps your child is hungry. Further, his blood sugar may spike and drop as a result of a diet that contains too many processed foods and sugars. Such a diet is guaranteed to make children irritable and whiny. Feed your children healthy meals and snacks at regular intervals—especially before you go grocery shopping to avoid the ever popular supermarket meltdown.

Frustration. When children begin learning more difficult concepts in school, such as grammar or math, they can become easily frustrated. This out-of-sorts feeling is not something they can explain other than to say something is too hard. Ask probing questions such as, "Honey, are you upset with school or with your teacher?"

Jealousy. The fear of being displaced by a new sibling sometimes makes children revert to acting like a baby and being needier than they really are. Try to carve out some one-on-one time, even if it's only fifteen minutes, so that your child knows he is still special.

Anxiety. The dread of a pending or suspected separation or divorce, a remarriage, or moving to a new home or school can all trigger whining.

Preoccupation with having fun. Many times kids whine because they are having fun and don't want to stop when you need to move on to your next task. Teach your kid how to ask for more time. "Johnny, if you want to play longer at the park, you'll need to ask me like this in your normal voice: 'Mom, can I play on the slide five more minutes?' If time permits, I'll consider it, but only if you ask without whining."

When asked what to do with a whiny child, some moms and dads offered the following strategies they've found to be effective:

- "When my younger children whine, I simply smile and tell them I don't speak that language—that I only speak English. I may have to repeat myself a time or two, but it works."

- "I ignore my children. At first, this just made them get louder and whinier, but when I explained that I would not listen to them or speak to them when they spoke that way, they quit in no time at all. Now I know that if they whine, there is definitely something else going on."

- "When my older children whine, I reply using pig Latin. They don't understand it at all and I won't share the secret. But it lightens the mood and the whining stops."

- "When our kids whine, we tell them to use their real words."

- "We use a chart with stickers to monitor how well the kids do their chores and live within the behavior and character expectations we have. Whining is one of the things that earns them a sad-face sticker. If you get three sad-face stickers for a single action in a week, you lose privileges. On the flip side, if they don't get any sad-face stickers, they are praised as being a nonwhiner and earn extra privileges."

Notice that in each of the strategies above, parents focused on changing their children's behavior using positive methods. However, I've heard of several *ineffective* approaches parents have taken to deal with whining. I'm only including them here so that you'll know *what not to do*:

- Whining back at them. You're trying to teach them to stop, so don't send a mixed message. Act like the parent rather than a retaliating playmate.

- Washing their mouths out with soap. While this may be effective punishment for using bad words, it seems inappropriate for whining.

- Spanking. I'm not saying spanking can't be effective and acceptable at times, but you want to stop the fussing and whining. You do not want to prolong it.

- Taping your child's mouth shut. This borders on physical abuse; steer clear of it.

These approaches focus more on the bad behavior the parent wants stopped rather than showing the right way to act. Instead, why not take a deep breath and remind yourself that the child is trying to tell you something.

The most important thing is to know that whining comes with the territory, but you can have a big role in minimizing it by teaching your kids how to communicate in a more direct and effective way.

Day 27

Bragging

*"What do you have that God hasn't given
you? And if everything you have is from God,
why boast as though it were not a gift?"*
1 Corinthians 4:7

Nobody, including God, likes a braggart. Bragging is
rooted in pride—that mind-set that takes personal credit
for the gifts, talents, and things that God alone has pro-
vided as a loving Parent. According to Proverbs 6:16-19,
a proud look tops the list of seven things that God *detests*.
This fact alone should be enough to motivate parents to
keep their children from becoming boasters.

Unfortunately, many of today's parents have gotten
caught up in praise-mania, desperately trying to make
sure their kids have strong self-confidence and high
self-esteem. They have unwittingly produced little self-
centered egomaniacs who have no sensitivity to other
people's feelings.

On one of my playdates with two of my favorite
eight-year-old girls from church, I gave each of them a
craft project. Allie, a celebrated high achiever, finished
hers in record time and was ready for the next activity.

She waited impatiently, stepped away a few minutes, and returned. When she could no longer stand the waiting, she exclaimed to the other little girl, "Are you still fooling around with that thing? I finished mine a long time ago."

I took Allie aside and explained to her that her quick mind was a special gift from God. I told her that she should not expect everyone to perform at her level because *she* had the gift. "There are people who have a special gift that you don't have," I said. "If you make fun or say hurtful things to people because they don't have *your* gift, one day someone will make you feel bad because you don't have *their* gift."

I believe she got the point. She is now seventeen, and I've never had to correct her in that area again.

Bragging is annoying and alienating behavior. Kids *and* adults tend to shun people who are always talking about what they do well or what they possess. Thus, it is important, at each stage of your kids' development, to employ specific strategies to keep them on the humble path.

You don't have to worry about toddlers, however. According to Dr. Vicki Panaccione, a child psychologist and founder of the Better Parenting Institute, toddlers are still developing a sense of who they are. And since they're working hard to master skills like talking in complete sentences and sharing, your praise and encouragement are crucial. "Kids this age need to feel secure, so that when they come across other people who are better at certain things, they'll still feel good about themselves."[7] She believes that boosting a toddler's self-esteem can make her less likely to be boastful later on.

Once your child passes the toddler stage, however, your anti-bragging campaign must become strategic. Teaching your preschoolers that bragging is not appropriate behavior is best accomplished by being careful how you praise them. Focus your accolades on *who they are* more than *what they do*. Children in this age group have an intense desire to please you, so center your compliments on admirable character traits such as sharing their toys and showing kindness to others. When praising them, be careful to avoid using such statements as:

- "You're the best."

- "No one is as pretty as you are."

- "You're the handsomest boy in your entire class."

- "No one can do this as well as you."

These extravagant expressions imply that everyone else is inferior or secondary. Now, when Little Johnny or Little Sally makes these same statements about themselves, the unwitting parent is appalled at such pride. As we discussed in chapter 13, "Giving and Accepting Compliments," when you build your children up this way, it turns them into performers. They find their identity in what others think of them. They do whatever they think is necessary to get praise and attention—including bragging and self-promotion. While it is okay to share their accomplishments with close family and friends, constantly boasting about your kid—especially in his presence—can set the stage for serious relational issues in the future.

School-age children who have been raised in a bragging environment typically notice things like who the smart kids are, who the athletic kids are, which girl all the other girls want to look like, and so forth. They do their own comparisons. This is the time in kids' lives when they need to learn selflessness and compassion. Further, they need to learn to be humble while being capable and to take joy in the accomplishments of others.

As a parent, you must be intentional in selecting your kids' extracurricular involvements. Not every activity should be one where there is a winner and a loser. Even in their competitive sports, caution them that winning isn't the end-all, that in life you win some and you lose some. Most importantly, teach them to lose graciously by congratulating the winner. I'm appalled at the hostility I've seen between the parents of opposing teams when I've attended my seven-year-old nephew's football games. Where is the model of a gracious loser?

When it comes to tweens and teens, we all know how fragile their confidence and self-esteem can be. They, like adults, often resort to bragging to cover up their insecurities. They try to make themselves look and feel better by climbing on a pedestal, hoping to convince others that they belong there—all the while feeling like an imposter.

If you see that your child is already developing a bragging spirit, here are some practical steps to cut it off at the pass:

- Lose graciously in adult sports, board games, or other competitive activities. And for goodness' sake, don't act like the world has come to an end when your child's team loses a competition.

- Make it a habit to compliment others (in the presence of your kids) on their abilities and good deeds.

- Involve your children in charity work and random acts of kindness. Show compassion for others (street beggars, needy families at church) and ask your kid to donate a cherished item to a disadvantaged child.

- Remind your children each day that you and their heavenly Father love them *unconditionally*—with no performance required.

- Teach your kids that people will find them more endearing because of their weaknesses or shortcomings than their strengths. Their strengths will be evident, so there's no need to call anybody's attention to them.

- Have your kid print out, post, and memorize this passage: "Let someone else praise you, not your own mouth—a stranger, not your own lips" (Proverbs 27:2).

Day 28

Teasing

*"The lips of the righteous know
what is acceptable,
But the mouth of the wicked what is perverse."*
PROVERBS 10:32 NKJV

A Bridgewater, Massachusetts, fifth-grade football team stopped teasing in its tracks in a very heartwarming and memorable way. When they learned that their beloved water boy, first-grader Danny Keefe, was being teased because of his speech impediment and for always wearing a jacket and tie (his choice), they went on the offensive. The team quarterback organized a Danny Appreciation Day and over forty students showed up dressed like Danny. They crowded into the Williams Intermediate School library cheering "Danny, Danny!" The local ABC television affiliate carried the story. "This is the best day ever," Danny said, beaming.[8]

Before you can teach your kids the limits and perils of teasing, you need to first help them understand the difference between teasing and joking. *Teasing* has several definitions, but the first one listed in most dictionaries uses the words *pester* and *annoy*. Next, it is defined as making fun of someone. When you compare that to *joking* (no, not practical joking), which is speaking in a playful or merry way that brings some level of delight to the target and others, you can see an obvious difference in the two. You must convey these differences to your children.

Once you've established a good understanding of funny, you should make humor a regular part of your family's life. When choosing the jokes and stories you tell or the movies you watch, make sure the humor is directed toward animals, situations, or the person directly involved and that it's not at someone else's expense. It's okay to laugh with your children when you tell them about the time Grandma outsmarted the rooster by crowing back at him, but it's not okay to laughingly tell about the time your sister froze on stage during the school play and everyone laughed at her.

If you notice or suspect that your child is teasing others, the first step in getting him to stop is to understand his core motivation. Here are a few "why do you tease" questions you might want to gently pose, depending on his age and level of emotional maturity:

- "In teasing Little Larry, were you simply trying to entertain others or make them laugh so they could have a good time? Even if it made Larry sad?"

- "Does it feel good to be the center of attention when you tease someone?"

- "Does it make you feel powerful or strong when

you tease others because you know you can get away with it?"

- "What do you think would happen if you said something good about the person you tease instead of something meant to make him look bad?"

Let your child know that picking on others is wrong, unacceptable, and will be met with strong disciplinary action. Admonish your kids to never engage in name-calling or teasing a person just because he or she is different.

At a recent conference, an author and speaker told me she had been called "Cyclops" when she lost her eye to cancer at age five and had to get a glass eye. I cannot imagine the humiliation she felt. Fortunately, she rose above it and today is in high demand as a speaker all over the world.

The Women's and Children's Health Network offers the following critical facts about teasing. You'll want to impress these upon your children:

- When teasing upsets someone, everyone around feels uncomfortable.

- Teasing is not okay if it hurts people's feelings.

- Having people afraid of you is not as good as having friends.

- Being the center of bad attention is not as great as being the center of good attention.

- If you tease others, then no one will stick up for you when you are teased.

- If you want to have friends, then you need to learn how to be a friend.

- There are laws against harassment wherever it takes place, and you could get into a lot of trouble.[9]

Now parents, don't stop with teaching the difference between teasing and joking or with making humor part of the dynamics of your home. Help your children develop a sense of honor by coming to the defense of those who are being teased, mocked, or ridiculed. Just as the fifth-grade football team stood up for Danny.

Plant and nurture in your children the courage and desire to stop teasing whenever possible. Explain to them that those who are happy and fun-loving have no need to laugh at the expense of others or to pull mean-spirited pranks on them. People who behave in this manner are almost always insecure, unhappy, and are looking to divert attention away from them and their problems or shortcomings.

These are not the kind of children you want them to be. These are not the kind of children you will be raising when you create both a loving and fun-loving home atmosphere.

As parents, you can make life more enjoyable for your children and their peers by teaching them that teasing will always be around—but it should never be associated with them.

Day 29

Verbal Bullying

*"Do to others whatever you would
like them to do to you."*
MATTHEW 7:12

In January 2013, Hailey Petee, an eleven-year-old
Ohio elementary school student, took her own life after
being bullied for over a year. According to her mom,
Melinda, Hailey was constantly bullied because she wore
glasses and struggled with attention deficit hyperactivity disorder.[10]

Gone are the days when the bully of the school was
one or two rough-and-tough boys. Bullying starts as
early as preschool, and both girls and boys are guilty of
being bullies. These days bullying is not only physical
but verbal and emotional. Student bullying is one of the
most frequently reported discipline problems at school:
21 percent of elementary schools, 43 percent of middle
schools, and 22 percent of high schools reported problems with bullying in 2005–2006.[11]

It is a huge problem, and most literature on the subject deals with how to respond or defend against a bully.
However, in keeping with my objective of encouraging

you to tame *your* child's tongue, this chapter will focus on what to do when *your* child is the bully.

Many parents are caught off guard as they naively assume that their kids would never be the perpetrator of such ungodly, antisocial behavior. It's time to stop making excuses and living in denial. If your child shows signs of being a bully, it's *not* just a phase. Kids bully for a reason and become progressively more violent and aggressive if the root of the problem is not discovered and addressed. If your child exhibits any of the following behaviors, you need to take action:

- laughs when others fall, get hurt, or get in trouble
- seems to take pleasure in observing violent or hurtful situations
- mistreats his toys and other belongings
- abuses family pets
- gleefully smashes bugs and worms
- hits or trips siblings or friends and laughs about it
- is frequently argumentative
- throws, breaks, or tears things in anger
- has few friends
- gets his way by using the "if you don't, I'll…" threat

Children who act this way are crying out for help.

They are angry, scared, frustrated, and often abused themselves. Their actions are usually *reactions*.

If your child displays any of these behaviors, don't stop at just calling it to his attention. Do some investigating to find out *why* he is acting out. Maybe a physical disorder could be the cause. Maybe he has been threatened or abused by a coach, teacher, neighbor, supposed friend, or family member. Perhaps he is being bullied and is afraid to speak up. Just maybe he is acting out in protest of a separation or divorce. Finally, he could be demonstrating the results of being allowed to watch or listen to violent, aggressive, and demoralizing television, movies, games, and music.

Let's look at some ways of preventing or redirecting your child away from bullying others.

Be clear about what bullying is. Don't let your kid excuse his bullying behavior by saying, "I was just kidding." Explain that physical fighting is not the only form of bullying. When your kids threaten, insult, relentlessly tease, or engage in name-calling, that's *verbal bullying*. Further, they are guilty of *emotional bullying* when they back stab, deliberately exclude a person from a group activity, or try to manipulate someone to do something against their will by making them feel guilty or ashamed.

The fastest growing type of bullying is *cyberbullying*. It involves spreading rumors or making threats using technology such as emails, text messages, Facebook, Instant Messaging, and sexting (sexually explicit messages or photographs). This all happens outside the purview of teachers and parents. Therefore, you'll want to be proactive and inform your kid that you'll be conducting a surprise audit of his computer activity from time to time to see if he is a victim or perpetrator of cyberbullying.

Seek to understand why he bullies. Ask your child leading questions that will help identify the reasons for his behavior. Ask, for example, "Are you driven by any insecurities (being too short, too tall, obese, from a poor family, not able to dress well, wanting to impress or be accepted by a certain group)?"

Also consider that a negative situation in your home may be triggering his desire to hurt others. Could your child be responding to verbal or physical abuse he experiences at your hands? Be honest with *yourself* as you seek to get honest answers from your kid. If he is feeling powerless to change his circumstances, he may seek to snuff the joy out of others.

A girl whose mother had passed away during the school year bullied me in the fifth grade because my family looked happy and functional to the outside world (it wasn't!). If your child is not forthcoming with his responses, seek outside help.

Ask your child to focus on understanding the victim. Is there a common description or profile of the types of kids he bullies? How does he select his targets? Have him explain in detail how he would feel if he were the victim instead of the perpetrator. Don't take "I don't know" for an answer.

Require him to apologize and make amends (when possible) to his victim. Don't demand that he say "sorry" if he doesn't mean it or show any remorse. (For more discussion on how to deliver an effective apology, see chapter 6, "'Sorry!' Versus Apologizing.") Notwithstanding, you can still require him to right a wrong with an act of kindness. Of course, the victim may not want any part of him going forward, but he will have done the right thing.

Despite using all the sensitivity you can muster as you work through these suggestions, *let you child know in no uncertain terms that you will not tolerate bullying*. Communicate to him exactly what privileges he can expect to lose (or other severe consequences) if you learn of any future bullying.

Bullying others has long-term negative effects on the bullied and the bully. According to the National Institute of Child Health, both are at greater risk of loneliness, lack of success in school, and becoming involved in drugs, alcohol, and tobacco. Further, 40 percent of boys identified as bullies in grades six through nine had three or more arrests by age thirty. Bullies are at a greater risk of suicide than their targets.[12]

Though I've focused on the bully, I cannot resist giving a word of caution to parents of the bullied. Please do everything possible to teach your kids to be assertive and confident. Most kids get bullied, not because they are different, but because they appear weak and defenseless, representing no threat to the bully. Kidpower (www.kid power.org), an international organization that focuses on kids' safety issues, offers great tips and practical exercises to teach your kids how to push back and not appear to be so vulnerable.[13]

Bullies have no regard for the fact that the "pitiful pup" they harm is God's child whom He loves. I know that many parents are in a dilemma whether to teach their kids to fight back or turn the other cheek. While God will avenge the wrongs perpetrated against His kids, I believe it is wise to teach your children to defend themselves from being hurt.

One biblical story that supports this is when Haman, a politically powerful bully, convinced the king of Persia to issue a decree to annihilate the Jewish people because he was upset with a single Jew who would not bow to him (Esther 3). When the king learned that his own wife, Queen Esther, was a Jew, he faced a dilemma. The law strictly forbade him from reversing the decree. So, at Queen Esther's request, he authorized the Jews to protect themselves from those who would try to harm them:

> On that day, the enemies of the Jews had hoped to overpower them, but quite the opposite happened. It was the Jews who overpowered their enemies. The Jews gathered in their cities throughout all the king's provinces to attack anyone who tried to harm them (Esther 9:1-2).

The Jews responded in self-defense. Enough said.

Day 30

Asking Inappropriate Questions

"Set a guard, O LORD, over my mouth;
Keep watch over the door of my lips."
PSALM 141:3 NKJV

Many years ago, our then eight-year-old godson, K.K., and I attended a wedding together. While waiting for the ceremony to begin, I struck up a conversation with a couple in their early fifties. After a few minutes, K.K., who was (and still is at age thirty) extremely personable and ever-curious, joined the conversation.

"Is this your husband?" he asked the woman.

"Ah, um, no," she said. "He's my boyfriend."

"Well, how long have you been together?" K.K asked, showing his surprise that such a seasoned couple wasn't already married.

"Twenty-eight years," she said with an obvious tinge of embarrassment.

I bumped his leg as if to say, "Stop the inquisition!" but he didn't get the message.

"Well, when are you going to get married?" he said.

Looking straight ahead, she tilted her head toward her boyfriend and said, "Ask *him*!"

Kids can ask the most ill-timed, embarrassing questions. Who hasn't heard a child ask such things as:

- "Why are you so fat?"
- "Why don't you have any hair?"
- "Why doesn't that man have two legs?"

Fortunately, most people will give young kids a pass since they understand they're not yet socially savvy enough to discern what not to ask. Unfortunately, when children get older, the questions don't always stop. Instead, they can become more personal:

- "Where's your dad?"
- "How much did that cost?"
- "Why won't your mom let you play sports?"
- "Why do you always wear the same pair of shoes?"

Children are naturally inquisitive. They want to know how, when, where, and—of course—why. That's a good thing. Further, you'd be surprised how many people are willing to engage in conversation with a kid to satisfy his curiosity. What an opportunity to learn to connect with people. Therefore, a child's inquisitiveness is not something a parent should try to extinguish. It is, however, something that needs to be nurtured and finessed at each stage of his development.

When a toddler asks an innocent but awkward question, it's best to just be cool and go with the flow. Like the time four-year-old Kathleen asked a lady at church if she'd stuck her head in the sink to make it colored like her mommy did. In these instances, a sharp reprimand is not the wisest response.

If the question isn't over-the-top rude ("Why are you so ugly?"), just get down to her eye level and either respond simply ("He's fat because people come in all sizes and shapes"), truthfully ("The lady is bald because she is ill"), or say something like, "We will talk about it later" or "That was not a nice thing to ask." Then let it go. If she persists, remove her from the situation, instruct her not to ask such questions, and then discuss the matter when the two of you are alone.

Older children—even those who are usually polite—will undoubtedly ask embarrassing questions from time to time also. When they do, it is perfectly acceptable for you to respond in various ways, including: "That's not something you ask someone." "If they wanted you to know, they would have told you." "That's not nice. Where are your manners?"

While there is no surefire way to prevent the occasional awkward or rude question from escaping the lips of your child, you can minimize the occurrence of those uncomfortable moments by talking about what is and isn't appropriate. However, stay mindful that children are children; they may not remember your admonition, so remind them frequently. Explain to them that all questions about personal finances, weight and physical features, and details about medical conditions are off limits. There are some questions children can appropriately ask their peers as they will come naturally to them as they form relationships with one another. However, the same subject is off limits with adults. For example, children should not ask adults their age (Grandma and Grandpa don't count).

Whenever possible, prepare your children in advance for potentially awkward situations. Say you and your children will be visiting a nursing home. Prior to the visit, explain to them that some people there might mistake them for their own family members, may want to hug them, might not smell very good, or may randomly talk, yell, or cry. Explain that their behavior is the result of being sick and unable to get well. Other situations to prepare for in advance include a visit to a homeless shelter, the addition of a child with disabilities to the classroom, meeting relatives you've not seen for a long time (or ever), visiting a different culture, and spending time with different ethnic groups.

Explain to your school-age children that an inappropriate question is one that is asked to make a point or to put someone on the spot rather than out of genuine interest or curiosity. For example, the following questions could be viewed not only as inappropriate but rude, depending on how they are asked.

- "Your family doesn't eat bacon—what's up with that?"

- "Why don't you like soccer?"
- "Do you ever get to see your dad?"
- "Do you have a dad?"

Instruct your kids *how* to verbalize their curiosity rather than shaming or punishing them for embarrassing you. Curiosity is a sign of an active mind, so encourage your kids to engage in their world. Teach them to preface potentially sensitive questions with "May I ask…?" This leaves the option for the other person to say he doesn't want to talk about it or doesn't feel comfortable in sharing. However, he might tell your child bluntly that it's none of his business. Either way, your child will have asked appropriately.

Parent coach Susan Stiffelman, author of *Parenting Without Power Struggles,* says that "most children don't intentionally want to make others uncomfortable; they are just intensely curious and have no way of expanding their understanding of the world without asking questions. While we do need to teach our children the fine art of discriminating between what is and isn't appropriate, it can be done with patience and kindness." [14]

Epilogue

Don't Try It Alone!

God is the ultimate parent. As such, He models an excellent balance of love, patience, and discipline.

"For the LORD disciplines those he loves,
and he punishes each one he accepts as his child."
(Hebrews 12:6)

No matter what circumstances brought you to the world of parenthood, God has honored you by allowing you to be a mother or father, or to serve in that role. Thank goodness He didn't leave you clueless. Rather, He has left a wisdom-packed Guidebook—the Bible—to instruct you on how to parent effectively. And He didn't stop there. He also left the Holy Spirit to empower you to do it.

What a generous Father! All that He is expecting is for you to acknowledge Him in all your ways so that He may direct your path as you parent the blessing He has entrusted to your care. Therefore, when your patience wears thin and you are tempted to go from one extreme to the other in your discipline (completely *abandoning* or totally *abusing* whatever "rod of correction" you've chosen), stop and reflect on how God has parented you. How often has He shown mercy when punishment was warranted, given you abundant resources that you did not deserve, and loved you even though you made bad choices?

Never give up on your child—and, for goodness' sake, don't try to parent alone. Reach out to your support system of relatives, friends, teachers, and coaches. Most of all, seek your heavenly Parent for help and guidance. Don't allow your hectic schedule and the cares of this life to stop you from running into your place of refuge. Be creative in getting there—like Susanna Wesley. Story has it that while raising the ten children who lived of the nineteen she birthed, she would often find a quiet place by simply sitting down in her kitchen and putting her apron over her head. Her disciplined children knew that she was praying and did not disturb her.

Where there is a will, there is a way!

More than all the practical suggestions in the preceding chapters, prayer will be your most effective tool for helping your children fulfill their divine purpose. With that said, I leave you this prayer and recommend you pray it often.

A Parent's Prayer

O Father, help me to treat my children as You have treated me. Make me sensitive to their needs and frustrations. Help me to listen with attention, insight, and understanding to what they have to say. Help me to treat them as a person of Your design and therefore of real worth. Help me to respect…their times to talk without interrupting or contradicting them…their ideas…their need for freedom to make choices and to take responsibilities, as they are able. O, give me the wisdom and understanding to teach my children as You have taught me.

Let me not forget they are children and not little adults, being patient and helpful as they are developing skills and mental abilities and allowing them mistakes and accidents without laughing at or belittling them.

Thank You for the provision of my need as a parent in charge of this flock of God. Thank You that in the Lord Jesus, You have given all that I need to be what I ought to be as a Christian parent.

Anonymous

Appendix

Child-Rearing Resources

- *Empowering Parents* (www.empoweringparents.com): Newsletter, articles, and blogs on a variety of parenting issues.

- *Inspirational Kids' Stories* (http://inspirational-kids-stories.com): A collection of children's bedtime stories by Daryl Grant that teach children morals and values.

- *FamilyLife* (www.familylife.com): Resources that offer biblical advice about marriage and parenting.

- *Focus on the Family* (www.focusonthefamily.com): Biblically based articles and advice on marriage and parenting.

- *Kidpower* (www.kidpower.org): Kidpower Teenpower Fullpower International (Kidpower for short) is a global nonprofit leader in personal safety and violence prevention education, serving millions of people of all ages and abilities across six continents. Kidpower focuses its teaching on violence prevention, bullying prevention, abuse prevention, and stranger safety.

- *KidSafe Foundation* (www.kidsafefoundation .org): This organization is dedicated to keeping children safe through prevention education programs created to decrease abuse, bullying, Internet safety issues, and abduction.

- *The Total Transformation Program* (www.theto taltransformation.com or call 800-291-5028): This award-winning, multimedia program for children and adolescents features the wisdom of child behavior therapists James and Janet Lehman. It provides a step-by-step plan for stopping defiance, back talk, lying, and disrespect.

Endnotes

Prologue

1. "16 House Rules by Susannah Wesley (John Wesley's Mom)," Raising Godly Children, March 28, 2011, www.raisinggodlychildren.org/2011/03/16-house-rules-by-susannah-wesley-john.html.
2. Chip Ingram, "Five Characteristics of Biblical Discipline," Focus on the Family, www.focusonthefamily.com/parenting/effective_biblical_discipline/effective-child-discipline/five-characteristics-of-biblical-discipline.aspx.

Part One: Training in Positive Communication

1. Stan and Jan Berenstain, *The Berenstain Bears Forget Their Manners* (New York: Random House Books, 1985).
2. Jill Rigby, *Raising Respectful Children in a Disrespectful World* (New York: Howard Books, 2012), 211.
3. Cherie Benjoseph and Sally Berenzweig, "Teaching Your Child to Say No!," www.modernmom.com/ad9c804e-3b35-11e3-be8a-bc764e04a41e.html.
4. National Crime Prevention Council, "What to Teach Kids About Strangers," www.ncpc.org/topics/violent-crime-and-personal-safety/strangers.
5. Betsy Brown Braun, "Excuse Me…and Don't Interrupt!," *Betsy Brown Braun* (blog), January 9, 2011, http://betsybrownbraun.com/2011/01/09/excuse-me-and-dont-interrupt/.
6. Chris Weller, "Children's Attitudes Toward the Disabled Improve with Contact; Can Be Direct Interaction or Observed," August 29, 2013, www.medicaldaily.com/childrens-attitudes-toward-disabled-improve-contact-can-be-direct-interaction-or-observed-254973.
7. Ibid.
8. Lisa M. Schab, quoted by Margarita Tartakovsky in "Raising Assertive Kids," www.psychcentral.com/lib/raising-assertive-kids/00011193.
9. C.M. Mueller and C.S. Dweck, "Praise for Intelligence Can

Undermine Children's Motivation and Performance," PubMed.gov, www.ncbi.nlm.nih.gov/pubmed/9686450.

10. Charles R. Swindoll, *Swindoll's Ultimate Book of Illustrations and Quotes* (Nashville, TN: Thomas Nelson Publishers, 1998), 76.

11. "Do the Prayers of Children Have Greater Impact?," www.cbn.com/entertainment/Books/WhisperingGodsEar.aspx.

Part Two: Triumphing Over Negative Communication

1. Stacie Bunning, "How Can I Stop My Child from Exaggerating?," www.greatschools.org/parenting/behavior-discipline/1487-stop-exaggerating.gs.

2. Wannikki Taylor, "Activities to Help Stop Kids from Exaggerating Stories," http://everydaylife.globalpost.com/activities-stop-kids-exaggerating-stories-17726.html.

3. Stan and Jan Berenstain, *The Berenstain Bears and the Slumber Party* (New York: Random House Books, 1990).

4. Timothy Jay, PhD, "When Young Children Use Profanity: How to Handle Cursing and Name Calling," www.earlychildhoodnews.com/earlychildhood/article_view.aspx?ArticleID=59.

5. "Telling an Adult About Bullying Isn't Tattling," www.peelregion.ca/health/bullying/pdfs/February-K-LPRF.pdf.

6. Tamara L. Chilver, "Teaching Your Child about Gossip," www.teachingwithtlc.com/2007/10/teaching-your-child-about-gossip_30.html.

7. Quoted in Marisa Cohen, "Brag-Proof Your Child," *Parents*, November 2007, www.parents.com/toddlers-preschoolers/development/social/brag-proof-your-child/.

8. "Suited Band of Brothers Stands Up for Unstoppable 6-Year-Old," November 21, 2013, www.wcvb.com/news/local/boston-south/suited-band-of-brothers-stands-up-for-unstoppable-6yearold/23085396/#!0XwN4.

9. "Teasing Others and How to Stop," Kids' Health, www.cyh.com/HealthTopics/HealthTopicDetailsKids.aspx?p=335&id=1625&np=286#1.

10. "Parents Say 11-Year-Old Daughter Was Driven to Suicide Because of Bullying," January 27, 2013, www.10tv.com/content/stories/2013/01/27/london-parents-say-11-year-old-was-driven-to-suicide-because-of-bullying.html.

11. Phil Nast, "Teaching Students to Prevent Bullying," National Education Association, www.nea.org/tools/lessons/teaching-students-to-prevent-bullying.html.

12. "Scared in School: Bullying Statistics," May 19, 2013, www.heraldextra.com/news/local/education/precollegiate/scared-in-school-bullying-statistics/article_74844177-1669-5ef5-9609-2c7234e92987.html.

13. Irene van der Zande, "Face Bullying with Confidence: 8 Kidpower Skills We Can Use Right Away," www.kidpower.org/library/article/prevent-bullying/.

14. Susan Stiffelman, "Ask the Parent Coach: Kids and Embarrassing Questions," *Huffington Post*, October 10, 2012, www.huffingtonpost.com/susan-stiffelman/kids-and-manners_b_1948505.html.

About the Author

Deborah Smith Pegues is an international speaker, award-winning author, a Bible teacher, certified public accountant, and certified behavioral consultant specializing in understanding personality temperaments. Her books include the bestseller *30 Days to Taming Your Tongue* (over 750,000 copies sold), *Emergency Prayers,* and *Choose Your Attitude, Change Your Life.* She and her husband, Darnell, have been married for over 35 years and live in California.

For speaking engagements, please contact her at:

The Pegues Group
P.O. Box 56382
Los Angeles, CA 90056
(323) 293-5861

Email: deborah@confrontingissues.com
www.confrontingissues.com

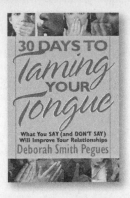

30 DAYS TO TAMING YOUR TONGUE
What You Say (and Don't Say) Will Improve Your Relationships

Certified behavioral consultant Deborah Pegues knows how easily a slip of the tongue can cause problems in personal and business relationships. This is why she wrote the popular *30 Days to Taming Your Tongue* (750,000 copies sold). Her 30-day devotional will help each reader not only tame their tongue but make it productive rather than destructive.

With humor and a bit of refreshing sass, Deborah devotes chapters to learning how to overcome the

- Retaliating Tongue
- Know-It-All Tongue
- Belittling Tongue
- Hasty Tongue
- Gossiping Tongue
- 25 More!

Short stories, anecdotes, soul-searching questions, and scripturally based personal affirmations combine to make each chapter applicable and life changing.

Also available is an interactive 30-day guide that will help readers think through how the book's advice can apply to their circumstances.

30 DAYS TO TAMING YOUR ANGER
How to Find Peace When Irritated, Frustrated, or Infuriated

From Deborah Smith Pegues comes an indispensable guide for overcoming anger and frustration. Using biblical and modern-day stories, Pegues helps readers identify the destructive habits that rob men and women of life's fullness and derail their personal and professional relationships. Readers will discover anger-taming strategies such as

- extending grace to others
- conquering perfectionism
- learning to laugh at themselves

30 Days to Taming Your Anger provides Scripture-based principles, heart-searching personal challenges, and faith declarations that point readers to a new sense of freedom.